Worship
with Fasting

An Insightful Look at a Forgotten Discipline

Albert Lemmons

To:
Bill & Donna
whose servant hearts we love,

Arthur & Patsy

PRAYERSHOP
PUBLISHING

Terre Haute, Indiana

PrayerShop Publishing is the publishing arm of the Church Prayer Leaders Network. The Church Prayer Leaders Network exists to equip and inspire local churches and their prayer leaders in their desire to disciple their people in prayer and to become a "house of prayer for all nations." Its online store, prayershop.org, has more than 150 prayer resources available for purchase or download.

ISBN: 978-1-970176-03-2

All Scripture quotations, unless otherwise indicated, are taken from the Holy Bible: New International Version. NIV, Copyright — 1973, 1978, 1984 by International Bible Society. Used by permission of Zondervan Publishing House. All rights reserved.

Scripture labeled "TNIV" is taken from the Holy Bible, Today's New International Version, Copyright © 2001, 2005 by International Bible Society®. Used by permission of International Bible Society®. All rights reserved worldwide.

Scripture labeled "NRSV" is taken from the Holy Bible, New Revised Standard Version, copyright © 1989 the Division of Christian Education of the National Council of the Churches of Christ in the United States of America. Used by permission. All rights reserved.

Scripture labeled "KJV" is taken from the Holy Bible, King James Version.

Scripture labeled "NASB" is taken from the Holy Bible, New American Standard Bible®, © 1960, 1962, 1963, 1968, 1971, 1972, 1973, 1975, 1977, 1995 by The Lockman Foundation. Used by permission.

Scripture labeled "NKJV" is taken from the Holy Bible, New King James Version, © 1979, 1980, 1982 by Thomas Nelson, Inc. Used by permission. All rights reserved.

Scripture labeled "GNT" is taken from the Holy Bible, Good News Translation, Copyright © 1992 by American Bible Society.

Scripture labeled "MNT" is taken from the Holy Bible, James Moffatt Translation, Copyright © 1922, 1924. 1925, 1926, 1935 by Harper Collins San Francisco. Copyright 1950, 1952, 1953, 1954 by James A. R. Moffatt.

Scripture labeled "AMP" is taken from the Amplified® Bible (AMP), Copyright © 2015 by The Lockman Foundation. Used by permission. www.Lockman.org

Scripture labeled "TLB" is taken from The Living Bible copyright © 1971. Used by permission of Tyndale House Publishers, Inc., Carol Stream, Illinois 60188. All rights reserved.

Italics in Scripture are the emphasis of the author.

Printed in the United States of America

Dedication

Arrayed in the beauty of holiness, Patsy Delores Davenport became my wife on September 11, 1955. She was and will always be God's perfect gift to me as wife and partner in my ministry. Her faith, spiritual passion and stamina have enabled us to serve our Lord together for more than sixty years. As I traveled around the world, she shouldered the responsibility of transforming five children into faithful adults. These children, along with their spouses, our eleven grandchildren and our ten great-grandchildren all rise up to call her Mother, Grammy and Blessed.

Patsy qualifies as co-author of all my work. Her typing skills are surpassed by none. She has made sense of my poor penmanship and lengthy sentences. She edits and rewrites my lessons and manuscripts with no shame. She is the denouement of my work and my life.

When from residence in the New Heaven we "remember" life as it was, because of his grace, we shall enjoy his presence together forever.

The last chapter of this book is a contemporary example and illustration of what led me to write this book. Our son, Stephen and his wife, Lynn, have experienced a forty-day fast from Ash Wednesday to Palm Sunday for the past twenty years. For five days most of those weeks, totaling almost 800 days, Stephen sat at his computer and poured out his heart. This addition is composed of a selection of his writings chronicling their spiritual journey. It is also a tribute to the man he has become despite the most severe trials.

Contents

Foreword 5

Introduction 7

Chapter 1: The Philosophy of Fasting 9

Chapter 2: Fasting in the Old Testament 17

Chapter 3: God's Chosen Fast (Isaiah 58). 27

Chapter 4: August Hermann Francke (1663–1727), Let the Hungry. . . .35
        Find Your Heart (Isaiah 58:10)

Chapter 5: Fasting in the New Testament. 51

Chapter 6: Alexander Campbell on the Subject of Fasting 63

Chapter 7: Questions and Answers on Fasting 77

    Additional Reasons to Fast 79

    Physical Aspects of Fasting 80

    Guidelines for Individual Fasting .81

    Guidelines for Collective Fasting .82

Chapter 8: Fasting, The Integration of Mind and Heart 83

Appendices 93

    From "The Philosophy of Fasting" Edward Earle Purinton, 1906. . . .93

    Proclamation Appointing a National Fast Day Washington, D.C. . . .94

    A Proclamation 95

Forty Days Fasting Journals . . . . 105.

About the Author 135

Foreword

May I tell you how I came to know Dr. Albert Lemmons? After serving a couple of years as a young preacher, the condition of the small church where we ministered discouraged me. We won no new people; we saw no impact on the little town and no enthusiasm among the members. I decided we should move on, so we headed to graduate school to look for answers and leave behind a failed ministry.

In the meantime, I realized I'd failed in ministry because I had failed to pray. I began to devour every book and seminar I could find on how God works through prayer, and that's when I came across the ministry of Dr. Albert Lemmons.

I heard him teach a prayer seminar in the late 1970's, then watched the videos of his lessons and read his materials. It amazed me that someone in our fellowship, the American Restoration Movement, had discovered this prayer-power which had eluded me, and that he taught on it with the same voice I'd heard in the old classics written about prayer. I didn't think anyone in our fellowship knew that much about prayer and fasting but Albert Lemmons surprised me, standing out as a pioneer among us in the spiritual disciplines.

In the late 1990's I met Dr. Lemmons at a church conference where he was teaching on prayer. At that time our congregation had just begun an annual Prayer Enrichment Workshop, so I asked him if he could speak on our program. He graciously agreed, and now speaks every year at our Prayer Workshop. For the last nineteen years he has taught classes at our workshop, mentoring our church and our guests by forcefully teaching on the spiritual disciplines of prayer and fasting. Many come to our yearly workshop just to hear him.

I've been honored to read his notes on this book during its writing. It projects a spirit, a quality found in all other classic books on prayer and fasting. It will stir your spirit. It challenges your conscience, pushing you to give quality time to building your spiritual life. It speaks with a voice that preaches holiness to a church desperately needing to reopen the wells of ancient spiritual practices, such as fasting.

In our hurried, self-indulgent era we've mostly forgotten about fasting as a spiritual discipline. Dr. Lemmons' book will break through the amnesia, awakening God's people to a new look at this ancient power.

Over the last few decades, Albert Lemmons has become a mentor to me. Like a spiritual father, he continues to encourage me to teach more about the spiritual disciplines. In like manner, he mentors our congregation charging us to keep hosting our annual Prayer Workshop. We have matured and grown spiritually deeper because of his influence and wisdom.

A preacher once told me, "When Albert Lemmons clears his throat, he gives you more wisdom than most people can by talking all day long." I agree. You will get a wonderful dose of that wisdom in this book.

Thomas Keith Roberts, D. Min.
Senior Minister, Calhoun, Louisiana

Introduction

The reality of an immortal spirit in each of us seems to have more far-reaching importance than the average person understands.

Whatever it takes to make the connection or create such awareness is valuable. If the fruit of one's life is any indication, and it is, then it may be that many who think of themselves as reasonably religious have yet to realize the thrill or excitement of encountering the abundance of blessing which may be derived from the practice of fasting.

The title of this book is lifted from the Bible itself. In Luke 2:37 it is said that Anna, a saintly eight-four-year-old prophetess, was the first person privileged to announce the coming of Jesus. She never left the temple but worshipped night and day, fasting and praying. In Scripture fasting and prayer are often connected, which implies that humility must also be a close friend.

In Acts 13:2, 3, Scripture says, "While they were worshiping the Lord and fasting, the Holy Spirit said, 'Set apart for me Barnabas and Saul for the work to which I have called them.' So after they had fasted and prayed, they placed their hands on them and sent them off." This narrates the beginning of Christian missions, and it is no accident that prayer and fasting were present. The first Christian community, whose life we feel throbbing throughout the pages of the New Testament, was one of joy and amazing wonder. The physical contact Jesus' disciples and friends had with him, no doubt, gave them a spiritual opulence and hope we cannot fully understand.

Jesus made it clear in his "departure teachings" that, although he would be with them afterward spiritually (see Matthew 28:20), he must leave them. They were assured that both an intangible and a tangible power would come to them after his ascension. That intangible power, or "*paraclete,* counselor," would be the Holy Spirit. This is a connection that has seldom been made, especially in our time.

In one of Jesus' most extensive teachings on prayer to be found in all of Scripture, Luke 11:13, he concluded by saying that the Father gives the

Holy Spirit to those who ask. Fasting, the tangible power, enables one to focus in ways beyond any other experience. Fasting assists in dealing with the human insoluble yearning. Therefore, if fasting enhances our asking, and God gives the Holy Spirit to those who ask, it follows that there is a potential filling of the Holy Spirit not to be had otherwise. This, I believe, was to be the tangible "substitute or otherness" so necessary in our lives to do what the personal presence of Jesus did for the disciples while he lived among them. The ultimate battle allows the spiritual capabilities of the human being to successfully rise above this physical existence. The final result—eternal destiny!

The purpose for writing this book is to show the ongoing battle between the flesh and the spirit. The matrix is food. However, Scripture allows for a broader definition. One of the most profound passages authored by the Holy Spirit was God's chosen fast of Isaiah 58—with little or no mention of food. The idea is making a choice based upon a greater value toward a greater goal: being forever in the presence of God.

This study is presented to confirm the foregoing premise. It is not intended to be a Reader's Digest version of the subject, but a principle reference work for the diligent student. May the Lord gift you through this grace and not allow the temporary to obscure the eternal, but to "taste the powers of the coming age." To God be all glory and praise.

CHAPTER 1

The Philosophy of Fasting

Edward Farrell, a leading contemporary author on fasting, penned the following:

> Almost everywhere and at all times fasting has held a place of great importance since it is closely linked with the intimate sense of religion. Perhaps this is the explanation for the demise of fasting in our day. When the sense of God diminishes, fasting disappears. Perhaps more accurately, when the vision fades, i.e., when the wisdom, language and tradition are no longer understood, the habit and practice wither away.[1]

Today one rarely hears the term fasting used in a spiritual sense. Why are modern-day Christians practically illiterate on the subject? Is it a lack of teaching, self-denial, self-discipline? Or is it a lack of intimacy and depth in our relationship with God?

Prayer with fasting as our Lord practiced and taught it becomes an important feature of Christianity. Prayer was the language of the heart of Jesus. It has also been the language of human hearts throughout the ages who seek a deep communion with God. Prayer needs fasting for its full growth and is the means by which we encounter the spiritual.

The first thought suggested by Jesus' words in regard to fasting and prayer is that only in a life of moderation and self-denial will there be sufficient heart and strength to pray much.[2] The church may have no greater challenge in her two millennia of existence than now. We enjoy so much affluence, have so much stuff to shuffle, that we do not need God anymore.

There is a fundamental issue: Why did God create bread and design you and me to need it to live? He could have made us like the angels in that sense. Why hunger? Why thirst? The battle continues to be between the flesh and the spirit. There is no finer line drawn in life than the voluntary discipline of fasting for a specified time in order to sharpen the edge of one's spirit in pursuit of God.

My spirit can hunger for God (celestial). The body hungers for food and thirsts for water (physical). God gave us these needs in order for us to appreciate Jesus as the Bread of Life (see John 6:35). The Bread of Life is spiritual food that endures until eternal life (see John 6:27). Jesus also quenches our insatiable thirst springing up to eternal life (see John 4:14). These physical bodies give us an opportunity to praise God in a way that angels may never know. Man was created with both the ability (power) and right (authority) to make a choice between the visible, which is temporal, and the unseen, which is eternal.

My definition of fasting is voluntarily giving up something good that is tangible in an effort to receive something better that is intangible. When one voluntarily subdues the physical in the interest of promoting the spiritual, there is a conversion process. "It includes focus, a clearer vision, a concentration on God. Fasting includes more than eating or drinking. What fasting really means, therefore, is abstinence from food to evoke the favor of God."[3] This is the battle in you and me. There are two kinds of hunger: physical and spiritual. I believe the secret in dealing with spiritual hunger is to manifest focused discipline of the physical hunger. When physical hunger is satisfied, one settles back in his easy chair and can eat no more. On the other hand, the more one satisfies his hunger and thirst for God, the more he craves.

One might expect Müller or Spurgeon, both constant communicators with God, as having reached their fill and not be spiritually hungry. Not so. These men and those in the Bible such as Moses, Samuel, David, the prophets, and the New Testament giants, were the hungriest for God.

If one does not feel a strong desire for the manifestation of the glory of God, it is not because they have drunk deeply and are satisfied. It is because they have nibbled so long at the table of the world that the soul is stuffed with small things, and there is no room for the great.[4]

Augustine said, "I fight, that I be not taken captive and carry on a daily war by fastings."[5] God challenges His people to awaken from the mundane and dulling effects of food—to say in effect, "This much, O God, I long for you and for the manifestation of your glory in the world."[6]

Fasting asserts the human will against the human appetite. In Romans 14:3–4 Paul is not specifically dealing with fasting, however, it could be included when he says, "Let not him who eats regard with contempt him who does not eat, and let not him who does not eat judge him who eats, for God has accepted him. Let each be fully convinced in his own mind" (Romans 14:5).

Jesus made it very clear that no one was to attempt to put the new wine of His Kingdom into the old wineskins of Israelite nationalism or old Jewish custom. He drew a distinct line of demarcation between Moses' instruction regarding the Day of Atonement (external form and ritual) with itinerant blessing. Marilyn McEntyre comments,

It is my understanding that fasting of any kind entails both spiritual and physical risks. It should be practiced under guidance to avoid temptations to unhealthy excess. Beyond these musings, I have begun over the past years to think about fasting in a new way: in a culture driven by endless cries of "more!" fasting can simply be a faithful affirmation of ENOUGH.[7]

Fasting is intensely personal though often practiced on a corporate (group) basis. I believe the new dimension Jesus intended by the "new wine, new cloth" concept is in a sense the manner of encountering and enjoying Christ's presence. God allowed me to understand many years ago that in one sense, the "God-kind" of faith is a means for approaching Deity. This allows one to see the unseen. "By faith he [Moses] left Egypt, not fearing the king's anger; he persevered because he saw him who is invisible" (Hebrews 11:27).

Faith stands on the finished work of Christ—the Lamb was slain, his blood was shed and that became the assurance *of things hoped for* (see Hebrews 11:1). As an act of faith, fasting is not denying food or God who provides it. Rather, it is when one chooses to pass up the gift to better know the Giver.[8]

Jesus' first words spoken in the New Testament regarding fasting were in the Sermon on the Mount. He had experienced a forty-day fast in the wilderness (see Luke 4:1, 2). When Jesus entered the wilderness, the Holy Spirit had already descended upon him at his baptism (see Luke 4:1). When he emerged from his forty-day fast, he returned in the power of the Spirit (see Luke 4:14).

It would appear that the potential of the Holy Spirit's power came forth in full manifestation after his fast. Fasting was the final phase of preparation through which he had to pass before entering his public ministry.[9]

The Sermon on the Mount has been called the constitution of the Kingdom of God. We believe that Jesus came into this world, lived, died, was buried and was raised from the dead on the third day (see 1 Corinthians 15:3–4). He concluded his earthly ministry by sending the Holy Spirit to reside in the hearts of his followers. He did this that we might desire to live out the Sermon on the Mount. It is only by the Spirit's power and guidance that disciples may experience a greater quality of life.

The Sermon on the Mount, found in Matthew, is divided into three chapters. Chapter five describes general qualities of Christian character. Chapter six begins with three spiritual disciplines as life is lived out in the presence of God. Chapter seven speaks about treasures on earth and in heaven and one's relationship to God.

God is Spirit. He responds to what we do in spirit and in truth. He sees what we do in the secret response of our spirit and then rewards us accordingly (see Matthew 6:18). During times of fasting, we allow ourselves to be drawn into his presence. Fasting has long been known as a means for intensifying prayer.[10]

The Sermon on the Mount is possibly one of the great landmarks in all of Christ's teachings. His physical journey as a man allowed him to see that the ultimate reward, heaven, is based on winning the battle between flesh and spirit. This is the doorway to enter from logical, rational, intellectual, religious life into a new world of righteousness and holiness without which no man can see the Lord.

Jesus said this happens when you give alms to the poor/ needy (focusing on *others*, 6:1–4), when you pray (focusing on *God*, 6:5–15), and when you fast (focusing on *self*, 6:16–18). The motive of the citizens of the kingdom of heaven deepens only as the law of *agape* love is embraced. Each of these disciplines is to be taken to heart, in the conscience of each believer. In turn it becomes a principle of character and conduct. This truth that our Lord is giving us principles, not laws, will appear more conspicuously according to the wisdom of the time or the wisdom of the man, or the wisdom of the church. Fasting is a focus of the heart. The sacrifice of personal will, which gives fasting its value, is expressed in the old term used in the law, afflicting the soul.[11]

For evangelicals, this whole question of fasting has almost disappeared from our lives and even out of our consideration. What place does it occupy in our whole view of the Christian life? The fact is that this whole subject seems to have dropped right out of our lives and right out of our whole Christian thinking. There is no difficulty in tracing the cause of that. It is obviously a reaction against so-called Catholic teaching in all its various forms. Our reaction has gone too far. However, our Lord presents it in the Sermon on the Mount, and we have no right to pick and choose which passages of Scripture we follow.[12] Fasting—Jehovah mandated it, kings proclaimed it, prophets preached it, and commoners practiced it. That should be enough to get our attention.

For millennia, church fathers have said there are two sacred sacraments or ordinances. Nowhere in Holy Scripture are baptism and the Eucharist mentioned in the same breath as sacraments; however, no one disputes their firm place in the ancient order. Webster's definition of sacrament/ ordinance as a direction or command of an authoritative nature, a custom or practice established by usage or authority, an established religious rite, specifically the communion. In Christianity, this applies to any of certain rites ordained by Jesus Christ.[13.]

Considering what Jesus said and did, there is a possibility of a third sacrament or ordinance in addition to baptism and communion. There is an eternal plan in the mind of God for his church. As God's plan came into being, it is obvious He had purpose and well-being in mind for all whose names are written in the Lamb's Book of Life. The Father created man with an earthly/fleshly dimension, but also with a spiritual capability. Man is not totally earthbound.

Jesus created and demonstrated three spiritual sacraments or disciplines. He was *baptized* of John in Jordan to fulfill all righteousness (see Matthew 3:15). After his baptism Jesus was led by the Spirit into the desert to be tempted by the devil. After *fasting* forty days and forty nights, he was hungry (see Matthew 4:1, 2). The benefit of the forty-day fast enabled the physical part of Jesus to stand strong against Satan. Satan left him and Jesus returned in the power of the Spirit (see Luke 4:14). The third spiritual discipline was the *Lord's Supper*, celebrated with his chosen disciples the night of his betrayal: "And he said to them, 'I have eagerly desired to eat this Passover with you before I suffer'" (Luke 22:15).

Thus we see that God's foundation for redeeming and sanctifying humanity is two dimensional: *physical* and *spiritual*. Both of these dimensions include the agent, the element and the recipient.

Baptism—two dimensions:

1. Physical: A human administrator (agent), water (element), and the body of the one baptized (recipient)—*born of water* (John 3:3–5).
2. Spiritual: Jesus (agent), the Holy Spirit (element), and the human heart (recipient)—*born of the Spirit* (John 3:3–5).

Fasting—two dimensions:

1. Physical: "After fasting forty days and forty nights, he [Jesus] was hungry" (Matthew 4:2).
2. Spiritual: Jesus addresses the heart of man directly, saying, "Your Father, who is unseen . . . who sees what is done in secret, will reward you" (Matthew 6:18).

Eucharist, the Lord's Supper—two dimensions:

1. Physical: Unleavened bread and *ampelos*, of the grape vine (fermented or unfermented).
2. Spiritual: By faith—"this is my body . . . this is my blood" (Matthew 26:26, 28); "do this . . . in remembrance of me" (1 Corinthians 11:25). "Remembrance of me" implies that the heart, the spiritual part of a person, is to be involved. "Examine yourselves to see whether you are in the faith; test yourselves. Do you not realize that Christ Jesus is in you—unless, of course, you fail the test?" (2 Corinthians 13:5).

Sacraments teach us one great principle: the righteousness of the citizens of the kingdom look toward God, who is its motive. Consider fasting, given by our Lord as the way in which we should conduct ourselves in the matter of personal righteousness.

Man is physical and spiritual. The body is the house in which the spirit lives. That "living soul" part of man has a potential for spiritual occupancy and is unique in all of God's creation: "to be made new in the attitude of your minds; and to put on the new self, created to be like God in true righteousness and holiness" (Ephesians 4:24). "May your whole spirit, soul and body be kept blameless at the coming of our Lord Jesus Christ" (1 Thessalonians 5:23).

God is spirit. The only way man can communicate with God is for physical ordinances to develop spiritual value. That which is born of spirit is greater and eternal. These God ordained ordinances have a physical element that decays as does the mind and body. Only the spirit remains eternal. The relevance and value of these sacraments are extremely important.

> **Baptism**—is a major subject in all biblical schools of thought. Jesus authorized it and was practiced by the early church. Peter, in 1 Peter 3:21, called it a pledge (*eperotama*) or prayer, thanking God for salvation by his grace.

> **Eucharist**—is the single cause for more discussion and disagreement over the years than probably any other subject. However, we know it is a principal New Testament teaching.

> **Fasting**—is rarely placed in the same reference of importance as baptism and communion. I wonder why. My purpose is never to over-emphasize or exaggerate any biblical teaching. One could well bring condemnation, or at least heavenly displeasure, to even attempt to do so. Indifference to eternal concerns is disgraceful. That is not the intention here.

The earthly ministry of the Holy Spirit began at Pentecost. On that day the person of the Holy Spirit was dispatched to earth to replace the person of Jesus. The power and authority of Jesus is still here, but is carried out in a way the physical person of Jesus did not (see Acts 2). Jesus assures all disciples that he will be with them until the end of the age (see Matthew 28:20). Preparing for his departure, Jesus was aware of the fear of the disciples (see John 14:1). They were more than upset. If Jesus was David's son, the Messiah, why, they thought, would he not defeat Rome? But the mission of Jesus was moral and spiritual deliverance, not physical or political. Jesus told Pilate, "My kingdom is not of this world" (John 18:36).

Why was it necessary for Jesus to return to heaven?

1. To personally take the sacrifice of himself to the Father, within the veil (Hebrews 6:19, 20; 10:19, 20).
2. To assume the role of high priest (Hebrews 2:17, 10:21).
3. To take his place at the right hand of the Father, making intercession for all saints (Romans 8:34, Hebrews 7:25). Jesus prepared his disciples from the time he left until he returns. The angel said, "As you have seen him go, so shall he return" (see Acts 1:11).

A divine role reversal occurred when Jesus returned to the Father and the Holy Spirit came to earth. The heavenly ministry of the Holy Spirit existed from eternity to Pentecost. He was the source of power/energy for *Logos* (Jesus before birth), and for prophets and all miraculous wonders of God until Pentecost. Upon the ascension (Acts 1:9–11), Jesus assumed his heavenly ministry (Revelation 5) and the Holy Spirit was the descended power on earth, as Jesus promised in Acts 1:8.

Jesus prepared his apostles and disciples for his earthly replacement. The promised Holy Spirit arrived personally on Pentecost and will remain here until the second coming of Christ. The person of the Holy Spirit is to anoint, indwell, lead, and be the earthly intercessor. "The Spirit himself intercedes for us with groans that words cannot express" (Romans 8:26). "No one can say, 'Jesus is Lord,' except by the Holy Spirit" (1 Corinthians 12:3). All gifts of ministry are given to men for Christian ministry. "All these are the work of one and the same Spirit and he gives them to each one, just as he determines" (12:11). The Holy Spirit is the element/gift that Jesus, the agent, utilizes in baptism (Matthew 3:11, Acts 2:38). Jesus is the Holy Spirit baptizer of all believers.

Fasting is the companion with the Holy Spirit to replace the person of Jesus on this earth—that's correct, fasting. While fasting relates to the physical component of humanity, the Holy Spirit relates to the spiritual component of humanity. Our whole being is meant to be spiritual, as governed by the Holy Spirit.[14]

Each believer is a child of God. Into the center of each heart God is now pouring his life, love and power. Through prayer and fasting we open our hearts to receive. Repetition deepens spiritual impressions. The practice of these gifts allows God to perfect his plan and purpose in our lives.

Conclusion

The attitude of Jesus toward fasting must be considered until he returns to earth. He practiced it for forty days as he launched his ministry (Matthew 4:2). He included it as one of three sacraments or spiritual disciplines in the Sermon on the Mount. He made it clear that following his departure his disciples would fast (Matthew 9:14–17; Mark 2:18–22; Luke 5:33–38). His teaching on fasting is in the same context of giving alms and prayer (Matthew 6:1–18). We would have no more reason to ignore or exclude fasting than to arbitrarily ignore or exclude the gift of alms and prayer.

Kingdom is more than we perceive with our senses. It is a call to look beyond the present and to allow the Holy Spirit to make the kingdom of God so real that it occupies first place in our aspirations. Fasting enables us to make the transition from a natural to a spiritual perspective. It is a deliberate choice to set aside the temporal in pursuit of the spiritual, or the voluntary subordination of the physical to the spiritual.[15]

"For the kingdom of God is not a matter of eating and drinking, but of righteousness, peace and joy in the Holy Spirit, because anyone who serves Christ in this way is pleasing to God and approved by men" (Romans 14:17, 18).

End Notes
Chapter 1 - The Philosophy of Fasting

1 Thomas Ryan, *Fasting Rediscovered* (New York: Paulist Press, 1981), 44.

2 Andrew Murray, *With Christ in the School of Prayer* (Gainesville, FL: Bridge-Logos Publishers, 1999), 102.

3 Madeleine S. Miller, *Harper's Bible Dictionary* (London: Harper and Row, 1952), 189.

4 C.S. Lewis, *The Problem of Pain* (New York: Macmillan, 1962), 102.

5 John K. Ryan, trans., *The Confessions of Saint Augustine* (New York: Random House, 1960), 120.

6 John Piper, *A Hunger for God* (Wheaton, IL: Crossway Books, 1997), 22.

7 Marilyn McEntyre, in *Weavings: A Journal of the Christian Spiritual Life* (Upper Room Ministries), Volume XIX, Number 5, September/October 2004, 41.

8 Piper, 44.

9 Derek Prince, *Prayer and Fasting* (Old Tappan, NJ: Fleming H. Revell, 1973), 80.

10 James Lee Beall, *The Adventure of Fasting* (Old Tappan, NJ: Fleming H. Revell, 1974), 22–23.

11 F.N. Peloubet, D.D., *Peloubet's Bible Dictionary* (London: Religious Tract Society, 1925), 195.

12 D. Martyn Lloyd-Jones, *Studies in the Sermon on the Mount* (Grand Rapids, MI: Eerdmans, 1971), 35.

13 *Webster's New Twentieth Century Dictionary of the English Language* (Cleveland and New York: World Publishing Company, 1956), 1259, 1593.

14 Charles Gore, *The Sermon on the Mount* (London: John Murran, 1900), 116.

15 D. Guthrie, *The New Bible Commentary Revised* (Grand Rapids, MI: Eerdmans, 1970), 858.

CHAPTER 2
Fasting in the Old Testament

In the ancient world, humanity in its desperation developed a gnawing inner sense of worship that included fasting. Their rituals embraced the extreme in an effort to appease the unknown. They devised every imaginable act of worship. They offered sacrifices to deities above and below, to the great and small, the sublime and ridiculous. They built monuments, pyramids and towers of all sorts, and they fasted. This act of homage has been practiced in all ages by all people and among all nations to express mourning, sorrow, pain and affliction.

The patriarchs from the beginning practiced the biblical discipline of fasting. It appeared to play a role in the mourning ritual of Abraham at Sarah's death (Genesis 23:2) and at Jacob's bereavement over the loss of Joseph (Genesis 37:34). The first recorded document addressing fasting is in Leviticus and is found in the section of regulations that accompanied the two stone tablets or ten words known as the Ten Commandments. In Leviticus 16:29–34, Moses established the Day of Atonement, a day of fasting, in the covenant between Jehovah and the children of Israel after God had delivered them from Egypt.

This day was important "because on this day atonement will be made for you, to cleanse you . . . from all your sins. It is a Sabbath of rest and you must deny yourselves" (Leviticus 16:30, 31). God established it as a "lasting ordinance" (16:29). It was a "holy convocation" (23:27 KJV). For a Jew the Day of Atonement is the holiest day of the year. It commemorates the day the high priest entered the Holy of Holies, in order to offer a yearly sacrifice for the forgiveness of the sins of the people.[1]

In order for this to take place, two important events had to occur: 1) Aaron, the high priest, had to observe ardent, specific rules on how to dress, what to do and when to do it in the Most Holy Place, and 2) all the people had to "afflict" or "deny" themselves.[2] There was a penalty for violation (Leviticus 23:28–32). Although nothing is specifically said about fasting in these verses, Luke refers to the Day of Atonement as "the Fast" (Acts 27:9 KJV).[3] Simply put, they were to fast. This was a lasting ordinance from God (Leviticus 16:31).

Fasting is abstinence from food, or the period during which it takes place. Involuntary fasting can arise from the fact that nothing to eat is procurable. Of this type were the forty days' fasts of Moses and Elijah.[4] The Hebrew words for this are *innah nephesh*, to afflict the soul or practice self-denial, to humble oneself.[5]

In many ancient cults, the practice of fasting was a national response to political or military defeats. Biblical accounts were primarily associated with expressions of grief and sorrow.[6] These emotions are often accompanied by a loss of appetite. Therefore, it would be most appropriate to connect or associate a spiritual benefit to fasting. If the origin was personal sorrow or grief as in the case of Abraham and Jacob, that would not diminish the evolution of fasting into a national or a religious rite by the time of Moses. This seems to have been the case.

The defeat of Joshua's men at Ai brought about such action as may be an exception. This action was not a part of an organized theological ordinance. Joshua's disposition of heart, along with that of the elders of Israel, seemed to meet any criteria for humbling oneself before God,[7] which David said he did by fasting (Psalm 35:11–14). The Hebrew Bible uses another word for fasting, *tsum* or *tzohm*. Simply defined, it means to cover the mouth or place one's hand over the mouth.[8]

The Day of Atonement was the annual expiation for all the sins, irreverence and impurities of all classes in Israel during the previous year. It was to be observed as a solemn fast in which they were to afflict their soul. It was reckoned a Sabbath, kept as a season of holy convocation (assembling for religious purposes), and persons who performed any labor on this day were subject to the penalty of death. It took place on the tenth day of the seventh month (corresponding to our October). This chapter, Leviticus 16, along with the words found in 23:27–32, were to be read each year publicly.[9] The Day of Atonement was God's affirmation that he had not forgotten the Jews—not forgiven, but not forgotten.

There was an additional reason for the absolute importance of the Day of Atonement, or Yom Kippur. In order for all Jews to enjoy right standing with Jehovah, an appropriation was to be made annually. Otherwise they would be charged as heathen. Romans 3:25–26 affirms that "God presented him [Jesus] as a sacrifice of atonement, through faith in his blood. He did this to demonstrate his justice, because in his forbearance he had left the sins committed beforehand unpunished—he did it to demonstrate his justice at the present time, so as to be just and the one who justifies those who have faith in Jesus." Moffatt's translation (MNT) puts it well: "in view of the fact that sins previously committed during the time of God's forbearance had been passed over."

This showed God as just in all history, up to and after the death of Jesus. He is now justifier, having made provision from eternity regarding the horrible domination of sin, to be forever obliterated. This is made clearer in Hebrews 9:15, as it related to the Jewish people, beginning with Abraham: "For this reason Christ is the mediator of a new covenant, that those who are called may receive the promised eternal inheritance—now that he has died as a ransom to set them free from the sins committed under the first covenant."

No person from Adam until the death of Jesus had their sins forgiven. The Day of Atonement was the means Jehovah chose to hold forth the sins of all Jews until the death of Jesus. That made "the fast," as Paul called it in Acts 27:9, important. The faithful Jews from Moses to the cross observed "the fast" on the tenth day of the seventh month, *tishre,* or October. "The Lord said to Moses, The tenth day of this seventh month is the Day of Atonement. Hold a sacred assembly and deny yourselves, and present an offering made to the LORD by fire" (Leviticus 23:26–27).

Fasting was important to the Jews in maintaining right standing with God. This was done until all sins from Adam until the cross were forgiven. In the one thousand years from Moses to the completion of the second temple by Zerubbabel in 516 BC, fasting had an important place in Jewish worship and life. One of the classic illustrations may be found in the instance where Jehovah said he communicated with Moses as with no other man. In one of the most sacred events ever for a mortal, Moses was in the mount with God for forty days and forty nights (Exodus 24:28). He was in awe of God (Deuteronomy 19:9). Moses was there a second time with the Lord for forty days and forty nights without eating bread or drinking water (Exodus 34:28). He was supernaturally sustained during that holy enclave. He was startled because of Israel's sin (Deuteronomy 9:18–19).

The men of Jabesh-Gilead retrieved the bodies of Saul, his three sons and his armor-bearer. Out of respect for Saul, "they buried them at Jabesh and they fasted seven days" (1 Samuel 31:13).[10] In this rigorous undertaking, they evoked the favor of God.[11]

One of my favorite prophets, Elijah, was a man like we are (James 5:17). In his strength of faith, he destroyed Jezebel's eight hundred and fifty priests. Because of his prayer three and one-half years of severe drought ended. His faith statement, "I hear the sound of a mighty rain on a cloudless day" (1 Kings 18:41), is still true today. Following those timeless exploits he fled from Jezebel. In his exhausted state, he prayed that he might die. "I have had enough, Lord," he said, "take my life." An angel of God was dispatched to Elijah with food and water (1 Kings 19:4–9). He traveled forty days and forty nights until he reached Horeb.

If the continued use of a sacerdotal principle reveals both its importance and necessity, then fasting in the Old Testament must be considered. In an effort to understand the overall benefit of this spiritual principle, the following categories emerge from the Old Testament:

First: Sorrow for Sin

1. For the director of music. A psalm of David. When the prophet Nathan came to him after David had committed adultery with Bathsheba. Have mercy on me, O God, according to your unfailing love; according to your great compassion blot out my transgressions. Wash away all my iniquity and cleanse me from my sin. For I know my transgressions, and my sin is always before me. Against you, you only, have I sinned and done what is evil in your sight, so that you are proved right when you speak and justified when you judge. (Psalm 51:1–4)

2. Then the Lord said to me, "Do not pray for the well-being of this people. Although they fast, I will not listen to their cry; though they offer burnt offerings and grain offerings, I will not accept them. Instead, I will destroy them with the sword, famine and plague." (Jeremiah 14:11–12)

3. So I turned to the Lord God and pleaded with him in prayer and petition, in fasting, and in sackcloth and ashes. I prayed to the LORD my God and confessed: "O Lord, the great and awesome God, who keeps his covenant of love with all who love him and obey his commands, we have sinned and done wrong. We have been wicked and have rebelled; we have turned away from your commands and laws. We have not listened to your servants the prophets, who spoke in your name to our kings, our princes and our fathers, and to all the people of the land." (Daniel 9:3–6)

The twenty-one day Daniel fast is an important topic in the overall study of fasting (Daniel 10:3).

Second: Deny Self

When I weep and fast, I must endure scorn (Psalm 69:10). Jehovah brought about one of the most amazing revivals of all history. Fasting evidently played a major role.

Then the word of the Lord came to Jonah a second time: "Go to the great city of Nineveh and proclaim to it the message I give you." Jonah obeyed the word of the Lord and went to Nineveh. Now Nineveh was a very important city—a visit required three days. On the first day, Jonah started into the city. He proclaimed: "Forty more days and Nineveh will be overturned." The Ninevites believed God. They declared a fast and all of them from the greatest to the least put on sackcloth...Do not let any man or beast, herd or flock, taste anything; do not let them eat or drink." (Jonah 3:1-5, 7)

Nineveh, the capital city of Assyria, responded in earnest penitence to the warning of total disaster from the messenger of Jehovah. A total fast was proclaimed throughout the city and God saw that they turned from their wicked ways. What did the Lord see that turned his angel of destruction from them? He saw a sincere, earnest corporate fast that covered the land. Humble repentance always brings heaven's mercy.

Depending on the precise dates of Jonah (circa 800 BC), one may establish the extent of God's mercy. It is generally understood that for two hundred years, or until 612 BC, Nineveh existed as a world power. Otherwise, within forty days she would have been an ash heap, a mound of stones upon which the wild jackal would roam. Repentance, combined with fasting, touched the heart of God for that wicked city.

Third: Act of Humility

David said, "I humbled my soul with fasting" (Psalm 35:13). Moses reminded Israel in Leviticus 16:31 that the Day of Atonement is to be "a sabbath of rest, and you must deny yourselves; it is a lasting ordinance." The New Testament reference in Acts 27:9 (KJV) called this a fast. From the days of Moses in all seasons of life, God's people "humbled their souls" by fasting.

When Cyrus authorized the Jews return to Jerusalem in 539 BC, Ezra proclaimed a fast, so that they might humble themselves before God and ask for a safe journey with all their possessions (Ezra 8:21).

Fourth: Soul-searching

In 2 Samuel 12:16-20, King David denied himself food and sleep as he prayed, wept, and fasted for the life of his child born to Bathsheba. This addresses the answer to the teaching of some that only the spiritually driven or morally pure are to fast.

David pleaded with God for the child. He fasted and went into his house and spent the nights lying on the ground (2 Samuel 12:16), perhaps thinking that he might gain favor with God. "My knees give way from fasting" (Psalm 109:24). He fasted before the child died, believing that while the boy was alive his prayer would be answered. His fasting was to enhance his petition. When the child died, he arose, embraced God's answer and continued his faith walk with Jehovah (2 Samuel 12:20).

Fifth: Discerning God's Will

Darius, the heathen ruler of Medo-Persia, fasted for Daniel's safety (Daniel 6:18). God would have spared Daniel with or without Darius' acts of contrition.

Sixth: Serious Decision

Esther records one of the many threats from political enemies plotting extermination of the Jews. "Go, gather together all the Jews who are in Susa, and fast for me. Do not eat or drink for three days, night or day. I and my maids will fast as you do. When this is done, I will go to the king, even though it is against the law. And if I perish, I perish" (Esther 4:16). Mordecai and the Jewish slaves of Persia entered a seventy-two-hour fast that Jehovah honored by reversing the balance of power in the Persian Empire. Esther became queen of the land and Mordecai became the prime minister. Haman was hanged.

Esther's story provides an excellent model for fighting our toughest battles. We see her following three important principles:

1. She settled in her heart that this battle was one in which she must be involved. She was in the palace *for such a time as this*. Her commitment was solid.
2. She called the Jewish people to a fast, recognizing that a solution was beyond her human wisdom. She would have to rely on God.
3. She took action one step at a time, expecting God's direction at each juncture.[12]

Seventh: Spiritual and Physical Revival

"Alarmed, Jehoshaphat resolved to inquire of the Lord, and he proclaimed a fast for all Judah. The people of Judah came together to seek help from the Lord; indeed, they came from every town in Judah to seek him" (2 Chronicles 20:3–4). Jehovah received their sincere fast. "Jehoshaphat stood and said, '... Have faith in the Lord your God ... and you will be successful'" (2 Chronicles 20:20).

Eighth: Continuation of Fasting

The love and loyalty of Jehovah's covenant with Abraham included provision, blessing and favor for the nation of Israel. "Surely the Sovereign Lord does nothing without revealing his plan to his servants the prophets" (Amos 3:7). The response of the people was to listen to the prophets of God and "diligently obey the Lord your God" (Zechariah 6:15).

Isaiah prophesized two hundred years before Cyrus the Great was born that he would decree that the remnant of Jews would return from Babylon and rebuild the city, Jerusalem and the temple (Isaiah 44:28). God called this Gentile king "my shepherd . . . and my anointed" (Isaiah 44:28, 45:1). The first group returned in 539 BC By 526 only the foundation of Zerubbabel's Temple had been built.

After seventy years, the people no longer remembered the power of God prophesied by Jeremiah: "This is what the LORD says: 'When seventy years are completed for Babylon, I will come to you and fulfill my gracious promise to bring you back to this place'" (Jeremiah 29:10). Upon the return, Haggai and Zechariah encouraged completion of the temple in 516 BC. "Ask all the people of the land and the priests, 'When you fasted and mourned in the fifth and seventh months for the past seventy years, was it really for me that you fasted?'" (Zechariah 7:5).

In times of national emergency, kings and prophets proclaimed special days of fasting to seek help and deliverance. Jehoshaphat (2 Chronicles 20:3) and the prophet Joel (Joel 1:14; 2:12, 15) are classic illustrations. Jeremiah made use of a day of fasting to have the words of the Lord read. "So you go to the house of the Lord on a day of fasting and read to the people from the scroll the words of the Lord that you wrote as I dictated. Read them to all the people of Judah who come in from their towns" (Jeremiah 36:6).

"In the ninth month of the fifth year of Jehoiakim son of Josiah king of Judah, a time of fasting before the Lord was proclaimed for all the people in Jerusalem and those who had come from the towns of Judah" (Jeremiah 36:9). Four annual fasts had arisen during the Babylonian exile. They were observed apparently without divine authorization.[13] These fasts had grown out of their own self-pity rather than from a consciousness of sin. Not only had they fasted unto themselves, but when they had eaten and drunk, they had done this also unto themselves. They needed to learn that men could not win the favor of God by fasting or by eating and drinking; neither then nor now can favor be won this way.[14]

Zechariah 8:19 addressed these annual fasts: "This is what the Lord Almighty says: 'The fasts of the fourth, fifth, seventh and tenth months will become joyful and glad occasions and happy festivals for Judah. Therefore love truth and peace.'"

1. The fast of the fourth month, Tammuz (July), was a general observance for the initial siege of the city, held on the day the city of Jerusalem was broken up by Nebuchadnezzar. The city was kept under siege until the eleventh year of King Zedekiah. By the ninth day of the fourth month, the famine was so severe that there was no food for the people to eat (see Jeremiah 52:5-7).

2. The fast of the fifth month, Ab (August), was held in response to Nebuchadnezzar setting fire to the temple, palace and the houses of

Jerusalem. "Every important building he burned down. The whole Babylonian army under the commander of the imperial guard broke down all the walls around Jerusalem" (Jeremiah 52:13–14).

3. The fast of the seventh month celebrated the death of Gedeliah by Elishama (2 Kings 25:25; Jeremiah 41:1–4). This was the third day of the seventh month, Tesri or Ethanim (October).

4. The fourth fast, on the tenth day of the tenth month, Tebeth (January), remembered Nebuchadnezzar and his army when they marched against Jerusalem (Jeremiah 39:1). Zechariah reminded the people that these four fasts were not for God, but for them (Zechariah 7:5).

The prophet made it clear that it is not fasting, but obedience, justice and kindness that are significant. The desolation of Judah was brought about by her disobedience.[15] Nevertheless, the prophet assured them that these fasts would be blessed with joy and gladness when they returned home and built Zerubbabel's temple, which was completed in 516 BC. "This is what the Lord Almighty says: 'Many peoples and the inhabitants of many cities will yet come, and the inhabitants of one city will go to another and say, "Let us go at once to entreat the Lord and seek the Lord Almighty. I myself am going." And many peoples and powerful nations will come to Jerusalem to seek the Lord Almighty and to entreat him'" (Zechariah 8:20–22). "Then the survivors from all the nations that have attacked Jerusalem will go up year after year to worship the King, the Lord Almighty, and to celebrate the Feast of Tabernacles" (Zechariah 14:16). Other public fasts were held when the Jews were threatened by any imminent danger.

"This is what the Lord says: 'Record this man as if childless, a man who will not prosper in his lifetime, for none of his offspring will prosper, none will sit on the throne of David or rule anymore in Judah'" (Jeremiah 22:30).

From the time Nebuchadnezzar deposed the Davidic lineage in 586 BC, the Jewish mind and heart were in exile. The construction of Zerubbabel's temple in 516 BC did not restore the rule of an approved monarchy. The Maccabean period failed in the effort. This explains the long-awaited desire for a king in Jewish tradition. This helps to answer the question to Jesus, "How is it that John's disciples and the disciples of the Pharisees are fasting, but yours are not?" (Mark 2:18). If you are the Messiah, you must destroy Rome. This is the end of Daniel's interpretation of the king's dream (Daniel 2:44). The time and place of Jesus fulfills Zechariah's prophecy: "This is what the Lord Almighty says: 'I am very jealous for Zion; I am burning with jealousy for her.' This is what the Lord says: 'I will return to Zion and dwell in Jerusalem. Then Jerusalem will be called the City of Truth, and the mountain of the Lord Almighty will be called the Holy Mountain'" (Zechariah 8:2–3). "Rejoice greatly, O Daughter of Zion! Shout, Daughter of Jerusalem! See, your king comes to you, righteous and having salvation. He will proclaim peace to the nations" (Zechariah 9:9–10).

Conclusion

The exercise of fasting consisted not merely in abstinence from food as far as health and other circumstances would admit, but also properly included humble confession of sin to God, with contrition or sorrow for them. It was an earnest appreciation of his displeasure and humble supplication that he would avert his judgments and an intercession with God for such spiritual and temporal blessing upon the Jews and others as are needed. The propriety of the practice of fasting may appear: 1) From divine commands given; 2) From many examples in Scripture; 3) in expressions of sorrow and a means of keeping the body in subjection.[16]

How scriptural is fasting? Listed below are examples of fasting in the Old Testament. A search through the Bible on the topic may help make up your mind as it relates to the three statements above:

- Genesis 24:33—Abraham's servant seeking a bride for Isaac.
- Exodus 34:28—Moses' first period of forty days on Sinai.
- Leviticus 16:29-31—on the Day of Atonement.
- Leviticus 23:14—fasting in offering of first fruits.
- Numbers 6:3-4—the law of the Nazarite.
- Deuteronomy 9:9-18—Moses' second period of forty days on Sinai.
- Judges 20:26—Israel after their defeat by Benjamin.
- 1 Samuel 1:7-8—Hannah's prayer for a child.
- 1 Samuel 7:6—at Mizpah under Samuel.
- 1 Samuel 20:24—Jonathan grieved at Saul's hatred of David.
- 1 Samuel 28:20 - Saul before his death in battle.
- 1 Samuel 30:11-12—Egyptian servant found in the field.
- 1 Samuel 31:13—death of Saul and his sons.
- 2 Samuel 3:35—David at Abner's death.
- 2 Samuel 11:11—Uriah's self-discipline in time of battle.
- 2 Samuel 12:16-23—David for the child of Bathsheba.
- 1 Kings 13:8-24—Prophet who cried against altar of Bethel.
- 1 Kings 17:6; 14–16—Elijah's restricted diet.
- 1 Kings 19:8—Elijah on his journey to Horeb.
- 1 Kings 21:4-5—Ahab after Naboth's refusal
- 1 Kings 21:9-12—Naboth set on high at Jezebel's instigation.
- 1 Kings 21:27—Ahab in self-humiliation.
- 1 Chronicles 10:12—those who buried Saul and his sons.
- 2 Chronicles 20:3—Jehosaphat before battle.
- Ezra 8:21-23—Ezra by the river Ahava.
- Ezra 9:5—mourning for the faithlessness of exiles.
- Nehemiah 1:4—for the restoration of Jerusalem.
- Nehemiah 9:1—Israel confessing their sins.

- Esther 4:3—Jews following Hamon's decree.
- Esther 4:16—before audience with the King.
- Esther 9:31—with the feast of Purim.
- Job 33:19-20—as a result of pain and sickness.
- Psalm 35:13—on behalf of others.
- Psalm 69:10—the cause of David's reproach.
- Psalm 109:24—physical results of extended fast.
- Ecclesiastes 1:13—sensing the heavy burden of life.
- Isaiah 58 3, 5-6—The Chosen Fast.
- Jeremiah 14:12—that which is unacceptable to God.
- Jeremiah 36:6-9—Baruch reading Jeremiah's scroll.

- Daniel 1:12-16—Daniel and companions refuse King's food.
- Daniel 6:18—Darius when Daniel was in the lion's den.
- Daniel 9:3—praying for Jerusalem.
- Daniel 10:2-3—Daniel's 3 weeks of partial fast.
- Joel 1:14—in view of the Day of the Lord.
- Joel 2:12—returning to God with a whole heart.
- Joel 2:15—proclaimed by blowing a trumpet in Zion.
- Jonah 3:5-9—proclaimed by the people and king of Nineveh.
- Zechariah 7:3-5—with mourning in the fifth and seventh months.
- Zechariah 8:19—fourth, fifth, seventh and tenth months.

End Notes
Chapter 2—Fasting in the Old Testament

1 John C. Wilhelmsson, *The Philosophical Contributions of Edith Stein, an Academic Thesis* (San Jose. CA: San Jose State University, 2016), 9.

2 Nathaniel Nicklem, *The Interpreter's Bible*, Vol. 2 (New York: Abingdon Press, 1880), 114.

3 Robert Young, *Analytical Concordance of the Bible* (New York: Funk & Wagnalls, 1910), 330.

4 John D. Davis, *A Dictionary of the Bible* (Grand Rapids: Baker, 1968), 229.

5 Francis Brown, S.R. Driver and C.A. Briggs, *A Hebrew and English Lexicon of the Old Testament* (Oxford: Clarendon Press/Oxford University Press, 1957), 776.

6 George Wigram, *Englishman's Hebrew and Chaldee Concordance* (New York: Oxford Univ. Press, 1970).

7 William Martin, *The Layman's Bible Encyclopedia* (Nashville: Southwestern, 1964), 245.

8 Ludwig Koehler and Walter Baumgartner, *Lexicon in Veteris Testamenti Libros* (Grand Rapids: Eerdmans, 1951), 719, 847.

9 Robert Jamison, D.D., *A Commentary, Critical and Explanatory on the Old and New Testaments*, (Glasgow, Scotland: S.S. Scranton Co., 1871), 85.

10 Orville Nave, *Nave's Topical Bible* (Chicago: Moody Press), 381.

11 Madeline S. Miller, *The New Harper's Bible Dictionary* (New York: Harper and Row, 1973), 189.

12 Quin Sherrer and Ruth Anne Garlock, *Making a Spiritual Warrior* (Ann Arbor, MI: Vine Books/Servant Publications, 1998), 197.

13 Charles Pfeiffer, *Wycliffe Bible Encyclopedia*, Vol. 1 (Chicago: Moody Press, 1975), 594.

14 Homer Hailey, *A Commentary on the Minor Prophets* (Grand Rapids: Baker, 1972), 356-357.

15 Jack P. Lewis, *The Minor Prophets* (Grand Rapids: Baker, 1966) 78.

16 John W. Parker, *The Bible Cyclopedia*, Vol. 1 (London: West Strand, 1841), 465.

CHAPTER 3

God's Chosen Fast (Isaiah 58)

―――

God's Chosen Fast by Arthur Wallis is a classic book on this subject for our present generation. Therefore it is appropriate to begin this chapter with his insight on Isaiah 58. Isaiah lived in a day when formalism and hypocrisy had rendered the religious exercise of fasting obnoxious to God.[1]

Isaiah lived in approximately 750 BC. In chapters 1–10, he denounced the lack of spiritual perception and the idolatry into which Israel had fallen. In any religious context when custom or practice replaces principle, the moral climate deteriorates.

There are some similarities between the days of Isaiah, Amos and our day. There was a deep call from within the human spirit, a yearning for God in a time of prosperity. All about them, and us, is a poverty of body and soul. Piety and form that overlooks the moral state of the poor has troubled God ever since Moses and probably since Adam. God began discussing that seriously with Moses and continued through John in the Apocalypse (Revelation 2:9).

Isaiah 58 is the greatest chapter on fasting in the Old Testament. The seven-fold fasting of Isaiah 58 follows a pattern: 1) the day for a man to afflict his soul to loose the bonds of wickedness; 2) undo the bands of the yoke; 3) let the oppressed go free; 4) to give bread to the hungry; 5) bring the poor and the hungry to your house; 6) when you see the naked, cover him and hide not yourself from your own flesh; 7) care for your own children.[2]

First is the type of fasting that God abhorred. It is detailed in verses 3–5:

"Why have we fasted," they say, "and you have not seen it? Why have we humbled ourselves, and you have not noticed?" Yet on the day of your fasting, you do as you please and exploit all your workers. Your fasting ends in quarreling and strife, and in striking each other with wicked fists. You cannot fast as you do today and expect your voice to be heard on high. Is this the kind of fast I have chosen, only a day for a man to humble himself?

Is it only for bowing one's head like a reed and for lying on sackcloth and ashes? Is that what you call a fast, a day acceptable to the Lord?

Other references to a degenerated spiritual state of the heart include Jeremiah 7:13 and Malachi 1:10:

While you were doing all these things, declares the Lord, I spoke to you again and again, but you did not listen; I called you, but you did not answer.

"Oh, that one of you would shut the temple doors, so that you would not light useless fires on my altar! I am not pleased with you," says the Lord Almighty, "and I will accept no offering from your hands."

The admonition of the Lord for the leaders then and now is to "set your heart to honor my name" (Malachi 2:2).

Covenant people of the Lord may fast, watch and pray, bow their heads like bulrushes in the wind, and lay on sackcloth and pour ashes on their heads (Isaiah 58:5). If however, they pursue only their own interests, if they allow injustice to continue and the needs of the afflicted to remain unmet, then all their outward faithfulness means nothing. God rejected as utterly hollow all religious show that neglected the needy.

Fasting in a fast food world is viewed as a dumb idea and ignored. Some think it is solely a throwback to Old Testament days. Stories of fasting by Moses, David, Daniel, Joel, etc. are expected, but for today? No way! Some may even look upon fasting as a means of manipulating or twisting the arm of God.

We make much out of imitating or being like the early church; yet fasting was often practiced by them. However, it was not the source of their fervor or passion. It merely enabled, encouraged and/or enhanced their intimacy with God. A word of caution: the act alone of abstaining from food does not make up for or alleviate malnourishment of the spiritual man. "More than any other discipline, fasting reveals the things which control us."[3]

Second, God's chosen fast in verse six is described by Isaiah. The first four statements address spiritual warfare.

1. loose the chains of injustice;
2. undo the heavy burdens, yoke;
3. allow the oppressed to go, be free;
4. break every yoke.

The four statements from verse 7 address social welfare.

1. Is it not to share your food with the hungry;
2. bring the homeless poor into your house;
3. when you see the naked, to clothe him;
4. do not turn away from your own flesh and blood?

What is the evolution of this moral matrix? The following strategies are set forth to develop this idea:

- Human energy and attention must be raised to such a level that there is a decisive direction dealing with chains of injustice.
- In undoing the burdens or removing the yoke, action items are set forth and met.
- In allowing the oppressed to go free, principles one and two have met their objectives.
- The idea of breaking every yoke may have been a clever way for the Holy Spirit to guide Isaiah in discussing the whole person.

These strategies provide for food, clothing, housing, etc. For every yoke to be broken is to assimilate the whole person into a new culture—the Christian community, the family of faith, the body of Christ. This is a process. The Holy Spirit moves each of us at our own pace. The objective is to take a poor, beaten-down human and move him along an ascending scale that presents him ultimately in Christ—mature (Hebrews 6:1–3).

This may be one of heaven's most important insights. We know that God loves and cares for people who love and care for people (Proverbs 19:17). This was not only the final apologetic of Jesus, but it was his main reoccurring word: "love one another."

One may ask, how is that a fast? The idea is that God's prosperity enjoyed among his people is a matter to be shared. The Scriptures say this again and again. This is the fast of God according to Isaiah, not from food but from too much of this world. The fast which God accepts includes self-denial shown in the exercise of justice, kindness and charity.[4]

God asks us to not only fast from food, but from life's pursuit of this world. He asks that in the emptiness created by this fast, we become filled not with our own luxuriant feelings, but with the crying need of the poor.

The affluence and the resources of the western world are wonderful blessings. It is much like Jehovah's blessing upon Israel when they entered the Promised-Land. They enjoyed prosperity. Moses gave a solemn warning before they crossed the Jordan that it would be difficult to remain humble before God. They would have houses they did not build, vineyards they did not plant and wine presses they did not dig. As a result their necks became thick and calloused and they forgot God who delivered them from the Egyptian yoke of slavery (Deuteronomy 32:15).

They were not prepared or equipped to handle the freedom and prosperity. Does this describe the present situation? Have we pushed God to the very rim of our agenda, to the edge of our lives? This explains why we cannot understand the fast of God about which Isaiah spoke.

The prophet Isaiah lived seven and one half centuries before Jesus was born. Early in his prophecy he spoke of the reality of the human state. He was reassessing Israel's Jehovah of yesteryear. He also had the courage to admit that a gulf had developed since the reign of King David.

"Chastening the soul is an essential part of faith and the means by which the human spirit reaches up to God and out to fellow man"[5]. There had been a deterioration of the worship of Jehovah, namely their understanding of "you must have no other gods before me" (Exodus 20:3). Since man becomes like the god he serves (Deuteronomy 4:15-19), the worship of the creation had replaced the worship of the Creator. This brought about a devastating change in the moral fabric of the nature of humanity.

In the same spirit that actuated Moses, the prophets bore testimony against the abuses to which the practice of fasting was turned in the lapse of time and with the increase of social corruption.[6] Gladstone once said, "Man should beware of letting his religion spoil his morality".[7]

God in his forbearance extended mercy and grace as a path for man to return to fellowship with God. The sacrificial elements of the first covenant enabled God to remember sin, but withhold his punishment. The nature of God's mercy is seen early in Mosaic instruction. Beginning in Exodus 23 and continuing to Zechariah many references pertain to caring for the poor. The Jews called the true fast the fasting of the heart.[8]

In a time of both spiritual yearning and societal distress, Isaiah made it plain: piety that ignored the needs of the poor would get nowhere with God. People might fast, pray devoutly, or bend like bulrushes in the wind. They might even cover themselves in sackcloth and heap ashes on their heads in a public display of devotion. If, however, they pursued only their own interests, if they allowed injustice to continue and the needs of the afflicted to remain unmet, then all their outward faithfulness meant nothing (Isaiah 58:3-5). Point blank, God rejected as utterly hollow all religious show that neglected the needy.[9]

From Matthew to Revelation the moral dilemma of the poor continued to be addressed:

- Blessed are the poor in spirit (Matthew 5:3);
- The poor shall always need the gospel preached to them (Matthew 11:5);
- Sell what you have and give to the poor (Matthew 19:21);
- Sold for much and given to the poor (Matthew 26:21);
- The poor widow cast in more (Mark 12:43; Luke 21:1-4);
- For the poor you always have with you (John 12:8);
- Has not God chosen the poor of this world? (James 2:5);

- Go, sell everything you have and give to the poor, and you will have treasure in heaven (Mark 10:21);
- Jesus told a story of a rich man in hades who ignored a fellow human's great need (Luke 16:19ff);
- In Luke 12, Jesus message about an uncaring attitude toward the poor must speak to us. Mere external observance of fasting is not acceptable.True fasting involves self-denial for the benefit of others.[10]

Is not this the kind of fasting I have chosen:
to loose the chains of injustice
  and untie the cords of the yoke,
to set the oppressed free
  and break every yoke?
Is it not to share your food with the hungry
  and to provide the poor wanderer with shelter—
when you see the naked, to clothe them,
  and not to turn away from your own flesh and blood?
(Isaiah 58:6–7)

The prophet strikes at the conscience and presses upon his hearers the inexorable demands of social justice, of sympathy and compassion, of love of neighbor and inward self-identification with him (Hosea 6:4–6; Ezekiel 18:5–9; 14–18; Zechariah 7:10; Job 31:13ff; Matthew 25:35–40).[11]

Share bread with the hungry, with those formally imprisoned. Bring the homeless and poor into your house, literally and otherwise. Do not ignore but extend fellowship to them. Care for the physically and morally naked. Replace self-worth, dignity and humanity to those whom robbers of life have taken from them. Do not hide yourself from them. We must develop community with those who have been deprived by bonds of wickedness. Jesus taught divide your bread with the hungry. The great fault of the human race is that people who have plenty frequently have faces of flint toward the poor, hungry, helpless and downtrodden of the earth.[12]

If you remove the yoke from among you,
  The pointing of the finger, the speaking of evil,
If you offer your food to the hungry
  And satisfy the needs of the afflicted,
Then your light shall rise in the darkness
  And your gloom be like the noonday.
The Lord will guide you continually,
  and satisfy your needs in parched places,
  and make your bones strong;
And you shall be like a watered garden,

> Like a spring of water,
>   Whose waters never fail.
> Your ancient ruins shall be rebuilt;
>   You shall raise up the foundations of many generations;
> you shall be called the repairer of the breach,
>   the restorer of streets to live in. (Isaiah 58:9–12 nrsv)[13]

These words must make us aware of the god of consumerism. Father of human spirits, may we have eyes to see and hearts to discern the subtle yokes by which our fellow earth travelers have been found. Help us to choose true freedom for them then we too shall be free. May your love and grace never be obscured from us as we not only hold the hand of the oppressed, but also as we embrace them with our heart.[14]

> Let us grow like our own ideals, and do
> The good which we have dreamed of hitherto;
> Or, if to things so high we may not reach,
> Lest we should miss the lesson God would teach,
> Let us forget our dreams and, day by day,
> Take up the common tasks about our way,
> And in these learn the secret of His will.
> We must not waste the golden hours, until
> Some nobler, greater task shall claim our care.
> He sends us forth a daily cross to bear—
> Sad hearts to comfort—lonely lives to bless—
> To help the widow, and the fatherless—
> To bring the outcast to our home, and feed
> The hungry poor who at our threshold plead.
> So shall the Christ-like be ours, and so,
> Unconsciously, our human lives shall grow
> Into the likeness of the life divine,
> And in the brightness of His glory shine.[15]

The result of the blessing of this fast 1) Your light shall break forth as the morning, 2) your healing shall spring forth immediately, 3) Your righteousness shall go before you, 4) the glory of the Lord shall be with you, 5) then you shall and the Lord shall answer, 6) you shall cry and he will say, 'Here I am,' 7) your light shall rise in darkness and you shall enjoy the noon day, the Lord shall guide you continually.[16]

A summary of Isaiah 58: When one strives to be spiritual, the constant battle of ritual versus reality is before him. It is much easier to go through the external forms of religion than it is to love God from your heart and allow the love of Christ to touch the lives of others.

What a difference it makes when serving the Lord, we have light instead of darkness, healing instead of disease, righteousness rather than defilement, glory and honor instead of disgrace. *Then life becomes a well-watered garden not dismal wasteland*, 11b.

END NOTES
Chapter 3—God's Chosen Fast (Isaiah 58)

1 Arthur Wallis, *God's Chosen Fast* (Fort Washington, PA: Christian Literature Crusade, 1968), 49.

2 Richard G. Moulton, *Isaiah* (London: Macmillan, 1898), Bk. 7, pg. 186.

3 Richard Foster, *Celebration of Discipline* (New York: Harper Collins, 1978), 55.

4 C.H. Irwin, *Irwin's Bible Commentary* (Grand Rapids: Zondervan, 1928), 260.

5 Gordon Cove, *Revival Now Through Prayer and Fasting* (Salem, OH: Schmul Publishing, 1988), 160.

6 Samuel Fallows, *Bible Encyclopedia*, Vol. 2 (Chicago: Howard Severance, 1906), 651.

7 John Morley, *William Ewart Gladstone* (London: Macmillan, 1903), 185.

8 H.D.M. Spence, ed., *The Pulpit Commentary, Vol. 10, Isaiah* (Grand Rapids: Eerdmans, 1950), 373.

9 Stephen V. Doughty, *Weavings* (Upper Room Ministries), Vol. XIX, 2004, 29.

10 John T. Willis, *The Living Word Commentary, Isaiah*, Vol. 12 (Austin, TX: Sweet Publishing Co., 1980), 447.

11 George A. Buttrick, *The Interpreter's Bible, Vol. 5, Isaiah* (New York: Abingdon Press, 1956), 680.

12 James Coffman, *James G. Coffman Commentaries, The Major Prophets, Isaiah*, 1 (Abilene, TX: ACU Press, 1990), 557.

13 Scot McKnight, *Fasting* (Nashville: Thomas Nelson, 2009), 111.

14 Elizabeth J. Carnahan, *Weavings* (Upper Room Ministries), 2004, 23.

15 Edith H. Divall *A Believer's Thoughts* (London: National Sunday School Union, 1906).

16 Moulton, 201.

C H A P T E R   4

Augustus Hermann Francke (1663–1727), Let the Hungry Find Your Heart (Isaiah 58:10)

Spelling and punctuation have been left as they appear in the original publication.

As a result of my many years of studying fasting, I view Isaiah 58 as the predominant chapter in the Bible exposing us to Yahweh's consternation. Its content is not so much about fasting itself, but more its connection with caring for the poor. This is the centerpiece of the heart of God (Proverbs 19:17). Other writers have had much to say on this topic. We read of Moses, Elijah and Jesus living out the practice in forty-day fasts. Isaiah emerged speaking with a voice of concern.[1]

Should it be a fast that I would choose, that a man humble his body on a day or hang his head like a reed or lay upon sack cloth and ashes? Would you call that a fast and a day acceptable to the Lord? But that is a fast that I choose, to let loose of that which you have bound wrongly, let free of those which you burden, set free who you oppress, tear away all burdens. Break your bread with the hungry, and those who are in misery bring into your house. Should you see one naked, clothe him and do not take delight in your flesh. Then your light will break forth like the dawn and your improvement will grow quickly and your righteousness will go before you and the glory of the Lord will take you to itself. Then should you call, the Lord will answer, if you should cry, he will say 'Behold, here am I. Thus you should oppress no one nor point your finger nor speak evil. And should you *let the hungry find your heart* and satisfy the wretched, your light will go up in the darkness and your darkness will be like noon. The Lord will lead you forever and satisfy your soul in the dryness and strength of your bones, and you

35

shall be like a watered garden and like a spring of water, which never lacks water. (Isaiah 58:5–11)[2]

From Moses to Paul, Scripture reveals the heart of God concerning His expectations of how man should conduct his life and share his wealth. "Make it your ambition to lead a quiet life, to mind your own business and to work with your hands, just as we told you, so that your daily life may win the respect of outsiders and so that you will not be dependent on anybody" (1 Thessalonians 4:11–12).[3]

In every culture and generation, humans have accumulated wealth—some by natural gifts, some by good fortune and some by inheritance. However, many others who have walked along the road of life are destitute and suffering.

God's concern is illustrated nowhere better than a story told by Jesus, a story obscured by the dust of millennia. It is time to lift its preserved and powerful message off the page and take a good look at its relevance today. The dramatic story of the rich man and Lazarus as recorded in Luke 16 is a final chapter in Jesus' life and shows his followers the true heart and value system of God.

Earlier in this chapter the parable of the unjust manager cannot be explained except to appreciate the shrewdness of Jesus in dealing with the world's values regarding money. "A shorter unit rebukes the attitude of the Pharisees and declares the arrival of a new era, which, though new, does not change the ethical standard God requires." Monetary resources, which possess a power to distort values, should be put to generous and serving use, so that heaven will be pleased to accept the one who has been generous.[4]

Jesus asks the question, "So if you have not been trustworthy in handling worldly wealth, who will trust you with true riches?" (Luke 16:11). This is important in understanding Isaiah's sermon to Abraham's children more than 700 years before Jesus. The special call and anointing of Moses must not be under estimated. He spoke the words of Yahweh. The heart of God from Moses, the prophets and the message of Jesus was this: God cares for people who care for people (Proverbs 19:17).

To become a disciple means to see for oneself the values that energized the life of Jesus of Nazareth, to struggle with them, until there comes that moment when by grace of God they become our own. Commitment to an ongoing and disciplined enrichment of our relationship to God, the affirmation of human need and worth in the face of the demonic pretensions of those principalities and powers that control our lives, the desire to serve life out of love rather than power or reward, and a deep identification with the poor and the hungry and the oppressed; these are values that we can see in the life of Jesus. They are values which when affirmed and lived will make a profound difference in the quality of life of the world that is emerging.[5]

The fourth principle of God's heart illustrated by what Jesus said and did is a deep identification with the poor, the hungry and the oppressed. This category may well include the financially wealthy. They too, are spiritually poor and desperate for answers found at the cross of Jesus.

In his final effort regarding generosity, the masterpiece of Isaiah 58 becomes more beautiful. Jesus' discussion of the rich man and Lazarus reflects certain ideas that were extant in Jewish thought. This story is not an effort to teach theology beyond the grave; however, it does that. He is stressing the need for right behavior in our time now. His stories never contradict theology regarding the Hadean world. There are other relevant passages to set forth those truths. I do not hesitate to make full use of the many implications of the rich man and Lazarus, the poor beggar.

There was a rich man who was dressed in purple and fine linen and lived in luxury every day. At his gate was laid a beggar named Lazarus, covered with sores and longing to eat what fell from the rich man's table. Even the dogs came and licked his sores. The time came when the beggar died and the angels carried him to Abraham's side. The rich man also died and was buried. In hell, where he was in torment, he looked up and saw Abraham far away, with Lazarus by his side. So he called to him, "Father Abraham, have pity on me and send Lazarus to dip the tip of his finger in water and cool my tongue, because I am in agony in this fire." But Abraham replied, "Son, remember that in your lifetime you received your good things, while Lazarus received bad things, but now he is comforted here and you are in agony. And besides all this, between us and you a great chasm has been fixed, so that those who want to go from here to you cannot, nor can anyone cross over from there to us." He answered, "Then I beg you, father, send Lazarus to my father's house, for I have five brothers. Let him warn them, so that they will not also come to this place of torment." Abraham replied, "They have Moses and the Prophets; let them listen to them." "No, father Abraham," he said, "but if someone from the dead goes to them, they will repent." He said to him, "If they do not listen to Moses and the Prophets, they will not be convinced even if someone rises from the dead." (Luke 16:19–31)

Who are those who by good fortune are obligated to help the poor? Jesus said, "A rich man who clothed himself in purple and fine linen lived every day in splendor and pleasure." It was he who was obliged to "do good" unto Lazarus. However, because of his neglect, he lifted up his eyes in the flames of his reproach and from the grave, he cried out. Likewise, we today have an obligation to the poor. One may ask, "Who are they?" Should people by themselves make decisions according to their own discretion about who is rich? The insatiable greed of the Western world does not qualify us to make that choice. So who should decide? The Word of God must be the judge. We go there for information regarding grace, salvation, security, eschatology, etc. Do we have the right to make a choice about feeding the poor? Jesus said there was a rich man. He did not give any details about how the man received his wealth. Perhaps his financial status was such that he did not need to work each day, thus allowing time to see after the poor beggar's needs. For most of us, Ephesians 4:28 describes the need to work that we may have something to share with those in need. Therefore does logic say that one who provides only for self is not godly-minded? If God's Spirit does not dwell in a man, can we say that he shares no mercy or love for anyone, much less the poor?

Back to the rich man—nothing is further said about him except that he died and went to Hades (hell, KJV). Has time changed this lesson? I don't think so. People who live selfishly, with no thought or action toward the poor, bear the same fate as the rich man. The name *Lazarus* means "one who has God as helper." God sent Lazarus to the rich man's door. This was a test for him, just as God tested Abraham to see how well he managed his possessions. Because man is addicted to self, we need the poor. We need them as an opportunity to give up things that perish in exchange for eternal or heavenly treasure. Demonstrating works through love is one way our faith is tested. When we hear of someone who needs food, clothing, or shelter, bear in mind that this is likely a "calling to account." May we remember that God entrusted us with this world's goods, not to hoard, but to share with the poor. When we falter, we must remember the rich man, who in the eyes of God was blamed for his lack of attention to the beggar. He clothed himself in purple and finery and lived every day in splendor and pleasure. According to Jesus, there was no excuse to set him free from Hades. Typical excuses may include "I worked hard for what I have; no one ever gave me anything." That attitude describes the rich man's mind set and heart. "In Hades, he lifted up his eyes" (Luke 16:23). That frightening reality clearly shows that all such worldly excuses avail nothing.

It is my prayer that Christians of all ages will be conscience-stricken because I think they have never thoughtfully rendered to their neighbor a true and useful service or consideration. This is especially true of those who have been blessed by God with an abundance of worldly goods. We must not think of possessions as ours, but be faithful stewards because it all belongs to God. He will require an accounting.

So what is the definition of rich? In the eyes of the world, the living standard of Western society is rich compared to those who are enslaved, starving, abused, unemployed, in poverty, etc. We may think only of gated mansions where multi-millionaires live as being the definition of rich. Not so. John the Baptist stated it rather clearly when answering the question, "Who or what is good fruit?" He answered, "The man who has two tunics [*kiton*[6]] is to share with him who has none; and he who has food is to do likewise" (Luke 3:11 NASB). The Apostle John later wrote, "But whoever has the world's goods and sees his brother in need and closes his heart against him, how does the love of God abide in him?" (1 John 3:17 NASB).

Do you believe this message is for you, for me, for today? According to the final sermon of Jesus, issues, right doctrines and liturgies, though they have their place, will not be the criterion for final judgment. Rather, His words in Matthew 25:37–40 say to us, "'When did we see you a stranger and invite you in, or needing clothes and clothe you? When did we see you sick or in prison and go to visit you?' The King will reply, 'I tell you the truth, whatever you did for one of the least of these brothers of mine, you did for me.'"

His admonition from the beginning of His ministry was Repent! Change your mindset or value system from that of this selfish world. His last admonition made it clear that at the second coming, the King "will sit on his glorious throne. . . . then the King will say . . . the King will reply . . . then He will say . . . He will reply" (Matthew 25:31, 34, 40–41, 45). In the above dialogue with all humanity, Jesus did not say that God the Lord would ask about church attendance, committee performances, and other sacerdotal matters. Rather, He will say, "I was hungry and you fed me. I was thirsty and you gave me to drink. I was a stranger and you took me in. I was naked and you clothed me. I was sick and you visited me. I was in prison and you came to visit me" (25:35, 36).

On the other hand, "Then he will say to those on his left, 'Depart from me, you who are cursed, into eternal fire prepared for the devil and his angels. For I was hungry and you gave me nothing to eat, I was thirsty and you gave me nothing to drink, I was a stranger and you did not invite me in, I needed clothes and you did not clothe me, I was sick and in prison and you did not look after me'" (Matthew 25:41–43).

Because of this inspired mandate from Jesus Christ, each of us must know in his heart that all of us are under a test of faith, no matter our financial status. Jesus spoke regarding the poor widow in Luke 21:1–4 after He watched her cast all she had into the treasury. His statement was, "She gave more than all the others!" They gave gifts to God, but this widow "gave her all." God is more interested in our sacrifice than the amount we give. Many give from their excess, which is not wrong as long as such giving is from the heart, and not from a sense of obligation.

Both the wealthy and the poor must properly use their many gifts. The manner in which one responds to opportunities for fellowship with the needy is a test of faith. Our love of God causes us to employ our temporal blessings toward a heavenly or eternal investment. This is why we need the poor worse than they need us. They are a "practice field" where we actively show God how grateful we are to him for his continuing provisions for us.

No one can exclude himself. Each one, no matter his place on the financial ladder, must observe his obligation to "all" the poor. A German pietist wrote, "For the Christian in church also sings the song of Jesus Christ our Savior thus: 'The fruits thereof shall not fail to come (to you).' One should care for his neighbor as your God has done unto you." He continued, "Now if a person is not thus minded to do unto his neighbor as God has done unto him, eating the Lord's Supper avails nothing." He referred to the hymn once more which said, "'the fruits thereof shall also not fail to come (to you).' You should love your neighbor that he can enjoy you as your God has done for you." But how has God done for you? He has given us his only begotten Son and with him everything (Romans 8:32). Because of his love for us our heavenly Father did not spare his only begotten son. We must not spare the best we have to show a lost world that we love them because He first loved us. As he laid down His life for us, so shall we lay down our life for the brethren (1 John 3:16). That means we should supply to and for them the necessities of life. That is a gift we owe.

When the heart is so unconcerned that one will not happily do to his neighbor what God has done for him, no real Christianity is practiced. John wrote, "God is love. Whoever lives in love lives in God and God in him . . . in this world we are like him" (1 John 4:16, 17). We who have received compassion and mercy from God will treat our neighbors accordingly. The question is often asked, "Who then is my neighbor?" Returning to Jesus' story, he said, "There was a rich man who clothed himself in purple and costly linen and lived every day in splendor and pleasure. But there was a poor man named Lazarus who lay before his door full of sores" (Luke 16:19, 20).

Here the poor man is called by name. The rich man's name is not mentioned. The memory of the righteous remains in blessing, but the name of the godless perishes (Proverbs 10:7). This is not the way of the world. God thinks and acts differently. In the world the rich and famous think they alone matter. Everyone hears about them and knows their name. In the end, there remains nothing left to say of them except that they were rich. God does not even record his name. On the other hand, the poor may be looked down on by this world, but they are dear to God. Who knows the name of that poor widow? Who knows the homeless and those in poverty? God knows.

Because of foolish or wicked deeds one may be without daily necessities of life. Even so, that does not excuse our attention, because we, too, have made bad decisions. If God waited for all men to be righteous before He allowed the sun to shine or give rain, it would never happen. God does not withdraw His blessings for our unrighteousness. He would have us imitate Him and show love and mercy not only to the worthy, but also to the unworthy. Indeed God would have us imitate Him and show love and mercy not only to the worthy, beloved and friends, but also to the unworthy who hate, curse, and persecute when they feel like it. Caution must be exercised to recognize deceivers who would take advantage of generosity; however, we cannot allow such conduct to be an excuse for closing the door on honest needs.

Ben Sirach in the apocryphal literature spoke the heart of Jesus when he said,

Let the poor not suffer need and do not be hard against the needy in their poverty. Do not cause the sorrowful an afflicted heart and do not record the gift to the needy. Do not deny the petition of the wretched and do not turn your face from the poor, for he who made him hears his prayer when he complains about you with a sad heart. Listen to the poor and answer kindly and gently. Act toward an orphan like a father and toward their mother like a husband. (Wisdom of Sirach 4:1–10)

Referring again to our main story line from Jesus, the rich man did not consider that Lazarus, who lay at his gate, needed a doctor to bind up his sores. As Lazarus remained there, the rich patron ignored him. Today there could be someone whom God has placed in your path, who suffers because they have not received the help they need. Most of us have the means to help relieve that distress. The spirit of Jesus of Nazareth will be resurrected among us when our world's goods are not used only for pleasure and luxury. Isaiah 58:7 says, "Bring the poor that are cast out into thy house" (KJV). Lazarus longed to be satisfied from the crumbs that fell from the rich man's table.

Evidently the rich man did not have to worry over that pitiful man full of sores who lay at his gate. Lazarus was so sick that he soon died. The rich man wiped his hands of the matter: "No more bother. After all, he's gone. I don't have to deal with that situation ever again." Oh, was he ever wrong! Can you imagine that unattended sores on a man at his gate would be sufficient evidence against him in the court of justice of the holy God for his spirit to be tormented forever? The lack of one temporal effort had eternal consequences.

The prophet thought it was a good idea to "break our bread with the hungry" (Isaiah 58:7). Lazarus longed to be satisfied "from the crumbs." For this reason we should not wait until we have more money. One should willingly share with others according to the gift that God has given, and desire to do more as we are able. When encountering a sick, poor, or needy person, take into account that you are looking into the face of the Lord Jesus Christ. Jesus said, "whatever you did for one of the least of these brothers and sisters of mine, you did for me" (Matthew 25:40).

If a stranger came to your door and you recognized him as the Lord, and he was wet, cold, and hungry, would you deny him entrance? Of course not! The Bible says we are bone of his bone and flesh of his flesh, members of his body. The respect we hold forth for the head should also be awarded toward members of his body. Each Christian heart must be disposed to care for each other as unto the Lord. "Therefore, as we have opportunity, let us do good to all people, especially to those who belong to the family of believers" (Galatians 6:10). Our counterparts 2,000 years ago were a great model for us. When they heard that a famine had arisen in Judea, "The disciples, each according to his ability, decided to provide help for the brothers living in Judea" (Acts 11:29).

The "poor of this world" extends much further than those in need of physical matters alone. The "spiritually poor" are also wretched. Their souls languish in fear, hopelessness and uncertainty. They may be ones who walked with their Lord for a while, but in the words of Jesus, "The cares of this world, and the deceitfulness of riches, and the lusts of other things" (Mark 4:19) have interfered with their Christian walk. They have leanness of soul; they may be considered the poorest of the poor. We are encouraged to snatch them from the fires of perdition (see Jude 1:23).

Jesus' words about trust and honesty are poignant. He merely illustrated by this story a heavenly principle that God holds before every man and woman: all worldly wealth and possessions are God's way of testing our faith. It shows where the Christian's heart really is. He said, "You cannot serve both God and money" (Luke 16:13).

If one does not use worldly wealth for ultimate heavenly results, the true riches, even heaven itself, will not be his to enjoy. All earthly wealth belongs to God. That is what the Bible says many times and in many ways. We are stewards; that's it and that's all there is to it. A steward is one who is charged and made responsible for the business affairs and property of another (1 Corinthians 4:1, 2 KJV). God will expose the motives of men's hearts as he judges us one by one.

And now the rest of the story. Scripture says, "And it came to pass that the poor man died and was carried by the angels to Abraham's bosom" (16:22a). Also it is written, "The rich man also died and was buried" (16:22b). Now he was in the flames of his own reproach. The Amplified Version (AMP) says, "Hades (the realm of the dead)." The Living Bible (TLB) says, "and his soul went to hell" (footnote: literally, "in Hades"). The Revised Standard says, "and in Hades, being in torment, he lifted up his eyes, and saw Abraham far off and Lazarus in his bosom. And he called out, 'Father Abraham, have mercy upon me, and send Lazarus to dip the end of his finger in water and cool my tongue; for I am in anguish (torment, KJV) in this flame'" (16:23, 24).

Immediately after death, the rich man realized his present and eternal plight. So long as a person is alive and sees someone in need, there is time to do something about it. When this physical life is over, the time of grace and opportunity is also over.

The rich man cried from the grave, and was given an answer: "There is a great gulf fixed" (16:26 KJV). His extravagant living and the good life just a few breaths ago are now gone and hereafter come hellish flames. In this life, the good life, his selfish life, he lived in splendor, but now and forever more he suffers with a dreadful thirst. Instead of the delicious drink that he had formerly enjoyed, he longed for even one drop of water with which the finger of Lazarus might refresh his thirsty soul. This was the poor, neglected man who lay at his door in life. We must realize from this that hellish torment rises up whenever a person is "unmerciful" in this life. The brother of Jesus wrote in James 2:13 (NASB), "For judgment will be merciless to one who has shown no mercy." The punishment of the rich man must have been especially horrendous when he could sense (see) Lazarus in his glory where the rich man could not go and was therefore to be deprived of eternal joy.

For the damned will see the salvation of the elect, but be dreadfully afraid, as He had not prepared them and they will speak to one another in repentance and groan in anxiety of spirit. This is he that we had for an example of mockery and derision. We fools thought his life senseless and his end shame. Now how is he numbered among the children of God and his lot among the saints? Thus we have missed the right way and the light of righteousness has not shone upon us and the sun has not risen upon us. We have gone on vain, false, and shameful paths and have walked wasted un-paths, but the way of the Lord we have not known. Now, how does our arrogance help us? Now what does our wealth together with pride bring us? All has gone like a shadow and like a runner that passes by forever. (Wisdom of Solomon)

The rich man's fate may also be considered a punishment for failure to show mercy while living. As a result all hope of being set free was cut off from the rich man. He was told that "between us and you a great chasm has been fixed, so that those who want to go from here to you cannot, nor can anyone cross over from there to us" (Luke 16:26). That is how it was and how it is. There is no hope in their hearts that could be delivered from ultimate hell. "And the smoke of their torment will rise forever and ever" (Revelation 14:11). They shall not have the slightest rest in Hades. Their conscience shall torment them and the torment will be increased through the observation of the others who will be damned, as Scripture continues to say in Revelation 14:11: "There will be no rest day or night." And as Isaiah says, "the worms that eat them will not die, the fire that burns them will not be quenched" (Isaiah 66:24).

In that circumstance the rich man was fixed in the flames of his reproach. Now in death, as in life, he first thought of himself. Then he said, "Then I beg you, father [Abraham], send Lazarus to my father's house for I have five brothers. Let him warn them, so that they will not also come to this place of torment" (16:27, 28). He had just been told, "Son, remember . . ." (16:25) and was reminded of his selfish life. His tormented conscience may have included selfishness toward his brothers. He may have been a role model for them, in such a way that he knew they were living just like he had. They, too, would ultimately be in his present situation, and that would intensify his torment.

Our failure to show due concern for Jesus' priority issues may be a wrong example that will influence others to fail even after we are dead. The statement "for their works do follow them" may not only be understood for righteous deeds but also for failure to hear the cries of the innocent and the tears in the eyes of hungry children. His spirit cried, "Somebody go and warn my brothers. Do not do as I have done and end up where I am. Do not come to this place of torment." He was answered from the grave, "They have Moses and the Prophets, let them listen to them" (16:29). This indicates a time period before or prior to the ultimate consummation.

Jesus makes a point that deserves attention. One may question him or argue with him, but Jesus said, "If they do not regard the message of God through Moses and the prophets, sending one back from the dead would not bring about genuine repentance. Jehovah has made it plain through all biblical history that he cares for people who care for people" (see 16:31; also Proverbs 19:17). This is *agape* love's highest priority. Everything else filters down from this.

Logical reasoning says if a sinner were released from *Tartarus* (hellish flames of reproach) to communicate with someone still in this world that would immediately change the way they live. Yet the Pharisees did not believe in Jesus Christ, even though they witnessed his many miracles including bringing some back from the Hadean world. His enemies acknowledged the miracles, but denied the power by which they were done. And their bitterness became more intense, as with all people who do not believe, Jesus said, for he would not even believe if someone came to him from the dead.

On the other side of that "fixed gulf" in Hades, stare, if you will, at the glorious reward of grace which the rich man could have enjoyed if he had observed his duty to Lazarus. What the rich man saw in Lazarus, who in life lay full of sores at his door, had now been borne of angels into Abraham's bosom. This is the one who in his few days of life and torment is now and hereafter comforted. This is assured to all whose priority is to follow Jesus as he encouraged us again and again to "visit the fatherless and widows in their affliction" (James 1:27 KJV).

This world is dead in its sin. A new birth is required for all those who would enter into life. Without this change, men and women are insensible to divine revelation. Through God's message of love there is a special drawing on the part of God to awaken the sleeping soul. Accompanying the new birth is spiritual vision—seeing the kingdom of God (see John 3:3). Faith is the means or work of God (see 6:29) for the reception into the soul of eternal life (see 10:28). The presence of eternal life, as a blessed gift, should remove much of this world's value system from our thinking and actions. This should cause us to think more about how may we use our few fleeting years and meager or much wealth on values which exist beyond our life. This may be what Jesus had in mind when he said use perishable treasure for an imperishable heavenly account. Do you think he was serious? Ask the rich man! Our "faith in God" (Mark 11:22) must manifest itself in imitating our Lord Jesus Christ. "As a person sows, so also shall he reap" (Galatians 6:7). If sowing was rich in love of God and neighbor, so will reaping be rich. Paul said, "Whoever sows sparingly will also reap sparingly" (2 Corinthians 9:6). Whoever does little good to the poor, will also receive little reward, and whoever sows blessing will reap blessing.

"They have freely scattered their gifts to the poor, their righteousness endures forever" (Psalm 112:9). Great joy may follow sincere mercy shown to a neighbor. First, one will be comforted as he departs this life. A compassionate one, like Lazarus, will be borne to Abraham's bosom and comforted. Even though he does not yet experience ultimate blessedness, the complete enjoyment of eternal glory, along with a new body, will come to him on the day of resurrection. In the meantime, he shall be comforted and finally bear the complete enjoyment of eternal salvation. This will be with all the redeemed for all ages in the New Heaven and the New Earth.

Another blessing of observing our Master's mandate of caring for the poor is that while here, the caring and obedient person becomes more and more like the image of God, for this is truly to be of God's mind. Holy Scripture speaks clearly when it says "do good unto all men" (Galatians 6:10). To have an uncompassionate, unmerciful soul which does good to one's neighbor reluctantly, or does not think of them, but cares only for self, is to bring condemnation. Too little has been said of the great mercy God causes to fall temporarily and eternally on those who practice mercy.

Jehovah God, through the treasured prophet Isaiah, describes the fast heaven approves.

> Is not this the kind of fasting I have chosen:
> To loose the chains of injustice
>   and unto the cords of the yoke
> To set the oppressed free
>   and break every yoke?
> Is it not to share your food with the hungry
>   and to provide the poor wanderer with shelter—
> when you see the naked, to clothe him,

and not turn away from your own flesh and blood?"
Then your light will break forth...
and your healing will quickly appear
then your righteousness will go before you,
and the glory of the LORD will be your rear guard.
Then you will call and the LORD will answer
you will cry for help, and he will say: Here am I. (Isaiah 58:6–9)

Those ancient words come alive! Seek your heart with all diligence. Find a place to serve, inquire, as you need. Once a small amount of time and money is shared with someone in need, joy will be your reward. Soon the spirit of narcissism of this present age will be broken. You will serve God with a new spirit. You will become rich in faith and good works (James 2:5, 1 Timothy 6:18). James continues, "because judgment without mercy will be shown to anyone who has not been merciful. Mercy triumphs over judgment" (2:13). Once one becomes rich toward God, benevolence follows; extend the hand of courtesy to those rich in this world's goods, but poor toward God, as well as all people in need.

Sirach said "first there are brooks, from the brooks grow great streams, from the streams grow great seas" (Wisdom of Sirach 24:44). When one begins to be merciful toward the poor, it grows and grows. Then your light will break forth to do even greater things.

The Pharisees also heard this message in Jesus' parable, but they were greedy and mocked him. Some who read this may think, "This guy phrases things well, and he knows he will receive enough money to do what he will. But others of us must provide for our own families and children. After all, Paul said if one does not provide for his own, he is worse than a heathen" (1 Timothy 5:8).

Be careful not to mock that advice to Timothy. Do not use it as an excuse or escape mechanism to excuse you from the Lord's will. Again I say, mock or excuse self if you will, if you cannot let go of it, you will speak to another of it on judgment day. "Then he will say to those on his left, 'Depart from me, you who are cursed, into the eternal fire prepared for the devil and his angels. For I was hungry and you gave me nothing to eat, I was thirsty and you gave me nothing to drink, I was a stranger and you did not invite me in, I needed clothes and you did not clothe me, I was sick and in prison and you did not look after me'" (Matthew 25:41–43).

We will see if excuses and the mocking of the Pharisees, 16:14–16, prevailed. Jesus continued to describe those who in lifetime lived out their faith in the living God. They cared for the wretched, poor, naked, imprisoned and needy. He honored them with his eternal presence. Those for whom faith is serious think willingly of obeying God's word. We repent and must stand in good conscience over what we have done in the past. The possessions we use to help others must not be given in the name of the Lord if they were obtained through dishonesty or deception. This would desecrate the Holy. Such wealth as comes by half-truths or thievery will not last to your third generation. Dishonest gains will fly away as fast as obtained.

The spirit of Zacchaeus is noteworthy: "Behold, Lord, half of my possessions I will give to the poor, and if I have defrauded anyone of anything, I will give back four times as much" (Luke 19:8 NASB). Ill-gotten gain is not a worthy gift to God.

We are commissioned, yet held accountable for the use of time as well as possessions. Our vaults are crowded with excuses. Our pantries indicate we are not sojourners, but permanent dwellers. Our settled-in approach to this life may reflect poorly on our view of the second coming of Jesus. It is a great victory—whoever is blessed let him enjoy. "For we brought nothing into this world, and it is certain we can carry nothing out" (1 Timothy 6:7 KJV).

If we have the necessities of life, let us be thankful. If God has blessed us with excess, it should be used for those who are without. Many parents have worked hard to amass money and property so that their children may own it when they die. So many times they use it unwisely, squandering what the parents have so greedily saved. When that happens, it is a curse and not a blessing. I wonder, I shudder, at the final accounting.

May we never use business as an excuse to pass by an opportunity to serve. Proper service includes relationships. Relationship involves time. It is easy to enable an addict or a disenfranchised person by handing them food or money. However, time spent with them would be beneficial in determining just how to best help. Seeing the heart of Jesus in your concern may be their only hope to know Christ and the abundant life.

"What good is it, my brothers, if a man claims to have faith but has no deeds? Can such faith save him? Suppose a brother or sister is without clothes and daily food. If one of you says to him, 'Go, I wish you well; keep warm and well fed' but does nothing about his physical needs, what good is it?" (James 2:14–16). The conscience tells us when we have sent away the poor man unclothed, unfed. "God knows your hearts" (Luke 16:15). Do not think as this world does. I know it is difficult, but Jesus said, "Sell your possessions and give to the poor" (Luke 12:33). George and Mary Müller did that at their wedding. We need to know their story of how heaven's bank opened up to care for them and more than ten thousand orphans in the sixty-four years of his ministry. Make your own "treasure in heaven that will never fail, and where no thief comes near and and no moth destroys. For where your treasure is, there will your heart be also" (see Luke 12:33–34).

By the Holy Spirit, Paul said, show me your sincere love. If you love God, because he first overwhelmed your heart with His love, you will be both eager and zealous to do much good. "Whoever is kind to the poor lends to the LORD, and he will reward them for what they have done" (Proverbs 19:17). If we would not be so selfish with our alms, so smitten with possessions, always dreaming of having more in the bank, we would be more like Jesus. Why do we think we need so much grain in our storeroom?

Command those who are rich in this present world not to be arrogant nor to put their hope in wealth, which is so uncertain, but to put their hope in God, who richly provides us with everything for our enjoyment. Command them to do good, to be rich in good deeds, and to be generous and willing to share. In this way they will lay up treasure for themselves as a firm foundation for the coming age, so that they may take hold of the life that is truly life. Timothy, guard what has been entrusted to your care. (1 Timothy 6:17–20)

Faith is a sure confidence of that in which one hopes and does not doubt that which one does not see (Hebrews 11:1). The faithful Christian has an invisible, living God in heaven. Trust Him. Remember He prepared food and drink before your birth. Now if God cared for you before you came into this world, He will surly care for you as you are in the world (see Matthew 5:25–34).

"If I speak in the tongues of men or of angels, but do not have love, I am only a resounding gong or a clanging cymbal. If I have the gift of prophecy and can fathom all mysteries and all knowledge, and if I have a faith that can move mountains, but do not have love, I am nothing. If I give all I possess to the poor and give over my body to hardship that I may boast, but do not have love, I gain nothing" (1 Corinthians 13:1–3).

See to it that you have a true love planted in your heart because it is God's *agape* love gift, fervently pray that He will pour out His sincere love in your heart. If you take your conversion and repentance seriously, God will have mercy on you. He will give you a sincere love for all the poor. When Christians use the earthly possessions as God intends, He will cause love to grow.

We cannot grow comfortable in the eyes of the world and become complacent, having such thoughts as, "I am a moral person; how then could I be in jeopardy and among those to whom He will say, 'Depart from me'?" Look back once more at the rich man. No one accused him of doing evil or of ill-gotten gain. He simply neglected to help Lazarus sustain life. Little would have been taken from his purse—not even enough to interfere with his life-style or his splendor.

Satan has also done a good job of blinding our eyes. Consider the houses we live in, the cars we drive, the clothes, bank accounts, even our pantry.

Do not neglect to do good. Imitate Christ, and even then, "when you have done everything you were told to do, should say, 'We are unworthy servants; we have only done our duty'" (Luke 17:10). Therefore, when you scarcely sow, remember, Whoever sows sparingly will also reap sparingly (2 Corinthians 9:6). However, if we intend to practice New Testament Christianity, ask God to give you the power to do so. You will reap great blessing and new love for God. Then, when Jesus comes, He will say, "Come, blessed child, you did it unto me. Come on; let's go home in our new heaven and new earth." Now, turn with me to God the most High and may we call humbly upon Him that He would seal His Holy Word by the message into each heart that it brings His fruit in us in active presence.

Prayer

Oh holy, eternal and living God and Father in heaven, to you be it humbly lamented that Christianity is so much dead among men that one can hardly still find a trace and sign of it. Ah, dear God and Father in heaven, forgive us by pure grace, as in our lifetime we have sinned from time to time against love toward our neighbor—left our neighbor without help and counsel. You are a faithful God. How often have you shown us Lazarus and we have not taken him in? How often have you caused us to hear the lamentation of the suffering and we closed our hearts to them? What would we say, Lord our God, as we are all guilty with one another before your face. Therefore we now ask you, forgive us our unmercifulness which we have practiced in our lives. But would you cause this, your Holy Word as is now proclaimed, to become right powerful in our hearts that we may not accept it as a mere outward exhortation, but rather that we consider, as you make clear to us, wherein true evidence of Christianity consists.

Oh, Lord, truly awaken each and every one who is now present and has heard this Word, that they all may know, taste, and feel something of your divine power and that they may let your Word work richly in their hearts as a right precious seed. As now your Word is richly scattered, give also that we may lay a right good foundation in all our hearts so that it may bear fruit, many a hundredfold, that we may prove our Christianity not with word or with tongue, but with deed and in truth.

Ah, faithful God and Father in heaven, awaken the hearts of men which are still so hardened. Ah, Lord! You see the wretchedness and the misery of those men who not only will not ever offer a hand to take in the wretched and suffering, but who even murmur against those who take them in. Ah, faithful God! Change our hearts; help that one even in our city may demonstrate a true, basic Christianity that we may no longer know of the poor and wretched who are stuck in need, but rather that instead through the abundance of those whom you have blessed in material things the poor may be helped in their need so that they are comforted and refreshed by us. For thus, O Lord our God, your judgment would surely be better prevented than through days of repentance and fasting, with which we only act the hypocrite before you in that we never begin to take the wretched into our house, to clothe the naked, or to give drink to the thirsty.

Ah, Lord! Give to us, that we may truly change and from now on receive a truly new heart and new mind, and because it is your mind, that you are love itself as you have described yourself to us when it says "God is love," ah, so help us by your grace, you who are love itself, that we may all experience in our hearts your divine mind, to love my neighbor as myself as you have commanded through our Lord Jesus Christ, who loved us unto death! Amen! Amen!

End Notes
Chapter 4—Augustus Hermann Francke (1663–1727), Let the Hungry Find Your Heart (Isaiah 58:10)

1 Many ideas and the translation of Isaiah 58 used in this paper come from Augustus Hermann Franke, a Pietist monk (1663–1727) who was a Hebrew scholar and a professor of theology in Halle, Germany.

2 This specific translation was read in 1697 at Glaucha in connection with his sermon, *The First Sunday After Trinity*. It is a sermon on caring for the poor. This sermon was translated by Gary R. Sattler, *God's Glory, Neighbor's Good* (Chicago: Covenant Press, 1982), 155–185.

3 Darrel Bock, *Luke: NIV Applications Commentary* (Grand Rapids: Zondervan, 1996), 418.

4 Bock, 420.

5 James C. Fenhagen, *Mutual Ministry* (New York: Seabury Press, 1974), 89.

6 n.a., *Analytical Greek Lexicon* (New York: Harper & Brothers, 1960), pg. 436.

More information regarding Augustus Hermann Franke, George Müller's mentor, may be found at www.prayermatters.org. and at Abilene Christian University's Special Collections Archive; The Albert George Lemmons' Papers, http://blogs.acu.edu/special collections. Dr. Albert G. Lemmons may be reached at 615-599-6091 or by email at patsylemmons@bellsouth.net.

CHAPTER 5
Fasting in the New Testament

There is background to why the disciples of John and the Pharisees were fasting with such diligence. The ministry of Jesus officially began with his baptism and the forty-day fast that followed. He and his followers did not fall into the same regimen of fasting as the Jews had for centuries. Criticism followed.

Yom Kippur had held the wrath of God off the Jews since Moses. The day of ornate fasting once a year was Jehovah's provision in his forbearance not to punish them for their sins. "For this reason Christ is the mediator of a new covenant, that those who are called may receive the promised eternal inheritance—now that he has died as a ransom to set them free from the sins committed under the first covenant" (Hebrews 9:15).

The presence of God requires holiness. When angels sinned, they had to be removed immediately. There could be no forbearance or probation in lieu of future expiation of sin. Because of where they were created they could never die, thus never be forgiven. God's unmitigated rule is death in consequence of sin. This accounts for Satan's presence in the Garden: "For if God did not spare angels when they sinned, but sent them to Hades, putting them into gloomy dungeons to be held for judgment" (2 Peter 2:4). This brings us to the sin of Adam and Eve. God created man in his image and likeness. He gave him a body of flesh in which his spirit dwells. He, unlike angels whose nature is spirit only, had both the ability and right to make a choice. The question arises, why didn't the holiness of God bring immediate punishment on Adam and Eve? In the mind of God, Jesus died before the foundation of the world (Revelation 13:8). Peter says, "You were redeemed with the precious blood of Christ, a lamb without blemish or defect. He was chosen before the creation of the world but was revealed in the last days for your sake" (1 Peter 1:19-20). Grace was given to us by Jesus Christ before the beginning of time (2 Timothy 1:9).

Moses was mediator of the Jewish covenant and Christ was ordained Redeemer from the beginning. In the heart of God, there was a cross for millennia before Calvary. God's forbearance demonstrated his justice by leaving unpunished sins committed before. Moffatt's translation (MNT) affirms that sins formerly committed during that time had been passed over. This showed God as a just God in all history up to and after the death of Jesus. He is now justifier because he made provision from eternity from the tyrannous domination of sin to be forever obliterated. Millions of sins over thousands of years accumulated against God. His grace allowed humans to appropriate right standing with God on a basis he prescribed until the death of Jesus (2 Timothy 1:9).

On behalf of Abraham's descendants beginning with Moses, God said, "'I will meet with you and give you all my commands for the Israelites'" (Exodus 25:22b; Leviticus 16:34). Jehovah's will for the Israelites was the Ten Commandments. The fast centered on the Sabbath which was divinely set apart in the Decalogue as a day of rest and worship. The Day of Atonement, October 10th, was known as Yom Kippur, a day of fasting. This was a day of humiliation and expiation for the sins of the previous year and was officially continued by Orthodox Jews until the destruction of Jerusalem in 70 AD.

This brings us to the mindset of the disciples of John and the Pharisees. From the destruction of Solomon's temple in 586 BC and their captivity, the Jews were without an approved ruler or king like David. Four fasts originated during that seventy-year period (Zechariah 8:18-19). The Jews thought fasting would encourage God to reinstate a Davidic rule in Jerusalem.

Six hundred years earlier, Jeremiah (22:30) said that Jehovah's resolve for the future did not include a Davidic type monarchy. This accounts for the stern rebuke, even criticism of Jesus by John's disciples and the Pharisees because Jesus and his disciples were not fasting. The forbearance and mercy of God held God's wrath from the Jews for fifteen hundred years. "For a Jew, the day of atonement was the holiest day of the year."[1] They knew the blessing of Yom Kippur. Jesus broke rank with them. He came to initiate a new concept regarding fasting. Thereafter the kingdom of God was not physical nor its headquarters in Jerusalem. It was spiritual. Jesus told Pilate "My kingdom is not of this world" (John 18:36; also see Hebrews 12:18-29).

Jesus began his ministry in this sacerdotal environment. Fasting in his life and ministry was not connected to the perpetuation of a misunderstanding of the true prophets of Israel (Isaiah 58:3, 4).

Some say, "I'm not into the prayer thing, I will leave that to someone else." What do you mean you are not into the prayer thing? Are you human? Even Jesus asks the Father for that "heritage of lost mankind" (Psalm 2:8). The only way God can give to Jesus his request is for intercessors "worshipping the Lord and fasting" (Acts 13:3) to activate the Holy Spirit. "He saved us, not because of righteous things we had done, but because of his mercy. He saved us through the washing of rebirth and renewal by the Holy Spirit" (Titus 3:5).

Jesus told his disciples that when he left them, God would send the Holy Spirit: "He will guide you" (John 16:13). When the people of God fervently pray and fast, he will dispatch angels to assist in accomplishing this supreme mission (Hebrews 1:14).

In terms of priority, prayer and fasting were among the important teachings of Jesus. One may ask, "How do you know?" We know by what he said and what he did. He fasted forty days following his baptism by John in the Jordan. The synoptic accounts, Matthew, Mark and Luke, give the most inclusive teachings regarding fasting in the New Testament.

The following scriptures are the words of Jesus:

When you fast, do not look somber as the hypocrites do, for they disfigure their faces to show men they are fasting. I tell you the truth, they have received their reward in full. But when you fast, put oil on your head and wash your face, so that it will not be obvious to men that you are fasting, but only to your Father, who is unseen; and your Father, who sees what is done in secret, will reward you. (Matthew 6:16–18)

Then John's disciples came and asked him, "How is it that we and the Pharisees fast, but your disciples do not fast?" Jesus answered, "How can the guests of the bridegroom mourn while he is with them? The time will come when the bridegroom will be taken from them; then they will fast. No one sews a patch of unshrunk cloth on an old garment, for the patch will pull away from the garment, making the tear worse. Neither do men pour new wine into old wineskins. If they do, the skins will burst, the wine will run out and the wineskins will be ruined. No, they pour new wine into new wineskins, and both are preserved." (Matthew 9:14–17)

Now John's disciples and the Pharisees were fasting. Some people came and asked Jesus, "How is it that John's disciples and the disciples of the Pharisees are fasting, but yours are not?" Jesus answered, "How can the guests of the bridegroom fast while he is with them? They cannot, so long as they have him with them. But the time will come when the bridegroom will be taken from them, and on that day they will fast. No one sews a patch of unshrunk cloth on an old garment. If he does, the new piece will pull away from the old, making the tear worse. And no one pours new wine into old wineskins. If he does, the wine will burst the skins, and both the wine and the wineskins will be ruined. No, he pours new wine into new wineskins." (Mark 2:18–22)

They said to him, "John's disciples often fast and pray, and so do the disciples of the Pharisees, but yours go on eating and drinking." Jesus answered, "Can you make the guests of the bridegroom fast while he is with them? But the time will come when the bridegroom will be taken from them; in those days they will fast." He told them this parable: "No one tears a patch from a new garment and sews it on an old one. If he does, he will have torn the new garment, and the patch from the new will not match the old. And no one pours new wine into old wineskins. If he does, the new wine will burst the skins, the wine will run out and the wineskins will be ruined. No, new wine must be poured into new wineskins. And no one after drinking old wine wants the new, for he says, 'The old is better.'" (Luke 5:33–39)

"The time will come when the bridegroom will be taken from them; then they will fast" (Matthew 9:15; Mark 2:18; Luke 5:33). Jesus drew a distinct line of demarcation between Moses' instruction and the parable of the new wine. The new wine of his kingdom was different from the old wine skins of Jewish tradition.

Even the idea of imposing the "old" on the "new" is unthinkable. No, "he poured new wine into new wineskins" (Mark 2:22). This described another dimension, or purpose for fasting in the Christian community. This new dimension included a "help" for the Christian prior to the second coming of Jesus Christ. "In the early Christian Church . . . fasting and alms were the wings of prayer."[2]

After his ascension, Jesus intended that his disciples fast for a different reason. Three times he specifically said, "and in those days shall my disciples fast" (Matthew 9:16, Mark 2:20, and Luke 5:35). While he was present with his disciples in a tangible form, fasting would have been an insult of inconceivable proportions as he viewed the "new" wine. The old wine idea dealt with pain, suffering, sin and loss. The new wine idea of Jesus included hope, joy, promise and expectation. After his departure, fasting would benefit his disciples just as his presence had done during his ministry. Jesus planned for something to act as a "substitute" or "otherness" on his behalf during his absence. He knew how important this was—after all, think of the magnitude of his solution!

The revelation of the mission and ministry of the *Paraclete* (Holy Spirit) waited for Christ's incarnation to be fully taught and his ascension made real, not just explained, but a reality (1 Peter 1:11b, Acts 1:2–11). On Pentecost, eight days after the bride-groom (Jesus) was taken away (Acts 2:1–4), the *Paraclete* (Holy Spirit) was poured out in a glorious baptismal measure. The divine energy resulted in Pentecostal power as the prophet Joel and Peter had recorded.

On the last and greatest day of the Feast, Jesus stood and said in a loud voice, "If anyone is thirsty, let him come to me and drink. Whoever believes in me, as the Scripture has said, streams of living water will flow from within him." By this he meant the Spirit, whom those who believed in him were later to receive. Up to that time the Spirit had not been given, since Jesus had not yet been glorified. (John 7:37–39)

The indwelling measure of the Holy Spirit could not be received until Jesus was glorified. "Concerning this salvation, the prophets, who spoke of the grace that was to come to you, searched intently and with the greatest care, trying to find out the time and circumstances to which the Spirit of Christ in them was pointing when he predicted the sufferings of Christ and the glories that would follow" (1 Peter 1:10, 11). The sufferings and death of Jesus paid the price for the glory that should follow. Jesus paid for everything on the cross. The Holy Spirit beginning at Pentecost would now be privileged to indwell believers. Sanctification (glory) could not happen until after the cross.

The primary teaching of Jesus regarding the person and work of the Holy Spirit is not found in his early ministry, but in a single discourse immediately preceding his crucifixion in John 14, 15 and 16. It is here that the disciples received a shock. Their hero, their source of physical and spiritual existence, announced his departure. Even their misguided ideas of his Messiahship were further dashed.

It seems more than coincidental that in his instruction on fasting, Jesus tied the coming of the Holy Spirit to his departure. The Holy Spirit and fasting were to nurture the disciples until Jesus returns. He makes use of the term "after my departure the Holy Spirit will come to you . . . the Father will send you another counselor/comforter, the Spirit of truth" (John 14:26). Some say "after my departure" referred to his death. His departure was included; however, the practice of fasting following his ascension attests to the truth that fasting was practiced by the early church for centuries. This is a parallel account of Matthew, Mark and Luke when Jesus said the bridegroom would leave and go to the Father. In verses 25–26, John affirmed that Jesus was still with them, but assured them that after the departure of the bridegroom the "children of the bride-chamber" will have the Holy Spirit as counselor. Jesus said the Holy Spirit would "infill" them with information they would need, just as he did when he was with them in his personal ministry. "I must leave," he continues, "to complete my Father's will, but I will come again."

In John chapter 15, he prepares his disciples for the inevitable transition, the inversion of roles. "You will be misunderstood, mistreated, unappreci-ated," he says, "but as children of the bride-chamber, you need not mourn." Notice verses 26 and 27: "When the Counselor comes, whom I will send to you from the Father, the Spirit of truth who goes out from the Father, he will testify about me. And you also must testify, because you have been with me from the beginning."

Paul casts insight in Romans 8:26–27: "In the same way, the Spirit helps us in our weakness. We do not know what we ought to pray for, but the Spirit himself intercedes for us with groans that words cannot express. And he who searches our hearts knows the mind of the Spirit, because the Spirit intercedes for the saints in accordance with God's will."

Fasting and the prayer of faith are catalysts to the "infilling" of the Holy Spirit thus giving access to the throne room of our Father. The absence of these practices may account for the lack of spirit-filled lives and spirit-filled churches in our time.

The practice of fasting following Jesus' departure deserves further discussion. Some have said that the statements of Matthew 9:15, Mark 2:20 and Luke 5:35 referred to the three days of his passion. It is certain that the fear of the unknown during the time of his death, burial, and resurrection may have been a special time of prayer and fasting for the disciples.

However, the place of fasting in the life of the early church after Pentecost discounts that idea. For centuries his followers fasted. Some classic illustrations follow:

- The Didache represents the preserved oral traditions whereby first century house churches detailed step-by-step transformation. The Didache reveals more about how Christians saw themselves and how they lived—and it does mention fasting. For instance, there is this passage: "and prior to baptism, let the one baptizing fast and let the one being baptized and any others who have the strength let them fast also."[3]

- Lyman Colman, 1796–1882 in his book *Ancient Christianity*, published in 1852, discussed fasting in the practice of early Christians.

  The practice of our Lord and his apostles respecting fasting may be thus described. Our Savior neglected the Jewish fasts to which the Pharisees gave scrupulous attention (Matthew 11:18–19). He represented such observances inconsistent with the genius of his religion (Matthew 9:14–18; Mark 2:15–22 and Luke 5:33–39). The practice of voluntary and occasional fasting he neither enjoined nor prohibited. Its use was necessary in certain cases (Matthew 9:15, 17:21). He fasted himself on occasion (Matthew 4:2). In practice, the apostles joined fasting with prayer (Acts 13:2–3; 14:23).[4]

- We learn from Justin Martyr that fasting was joined with prayer at Ephesus and in the administration of baptism. In the second century in the time of Victor and Irenaeus it had become usual to fast before

Easter. Clement of Alexandria speaks of weekly fasts. Tertullian complains heavily of the little attention paid by the Catholic Church to fasting. Origen discusses fasting in his tenth homily on Leviticus.[5]

- "The custom of the church at the end of the fourth century may be collected from Epiphanius. The entire Christian church practiced fast days throughout the year. Practice by the Second Canon of Orleans, AD 541, was regarded as important. Neglect could cause one to be treated as an offender against the laws of the church. The eighth council of Toledo condemns any who should eat flesh during the fast before Easter. This extended into the seventh century."[6]

In John 14:26 Jesus said, "'But the Counselor, which is the Holy Spirit, whom the Father will send in my name, will teach you all things and will remind you of everything I have said to you. I must leave in order that the Holy Spirit may descend." This was a great inversion of roles. Jesus personally left earth and joined his Father. The Holy Spirit left the right hand presence of God in heaven and came to earth on Pentecost. He will remain here until the final consummation.

How were the disciples of Jesus to receive this magnificent gift both then and now? In one of the most informative passages on prayer Jesus ever taught, he concluded his discussion in Luke 11:13 on an emotional note. He taught the importance and desire of mortals giving good gifts to their children. How much more will your Father in heaven give the Holy Spirit to those who ask him? The tense of the verb suggests a future request in prayer.

My definition of fasting is "voluntarily giving up something good in order to achieve something better." In authentic fasting, there is a potential conversion of power from the physical to the spiritual. Since fasting ennobles asking, is it possible that in fasting there is the possibility of being filled with the Holy Spirit in a measure not to be had otherwise? The ministry of the Paraclete (Holy Spirit) in one's life is the result of the prayer of faith, and is best achieved through fasting.

Fasting in the Life of Paul

Prayer and fasting were sacred truths regarding the conversion of Saul of Tarsus. Upon God's call on his life, Saul, the sinner prayed, "Who are you Lord'?" His answer: "I am Jesus, whom you are persecuting" (Acts 9:4, 5). "For three days he was blind, and did not eat or drink anything. . . . Then Ananias went to the house and entered it. Placing his hands on Saul, he said, 'Brother Saul, the Lord Jesus, who appeared to you on the road as you were coming here, has sent me so that you may see again and be filled with the Holy Spirit.' Immediately, something like scales fell from Saul's eyes, and he could see again. He got up and was baptized" (Acts 9:9, 17, 18). Prayer and fasting were included in the conversion of Paul, the great martyr, as he became a missionary. His life cannot be understood apart from prayer and fasting. See, for example, 2 Corinthians 6:1, 3–5 (KJV): "We then, as workers together with him, beseech you also that ye receive not the grace of God in vain. But in all things approving ourselves as the ministers of God, in much patience, in afflictions, in necessities, in distresses, in stripes, in imprisonments, in tumults, in labours, in watchings, in fastings."

Notice also 2 Corinthians 11:22, 23, 27 (KJV): "Are they Hebrews? so am I. Are they Israelites? so am I. Are they the seed of Abraham? so am I. Are they ministers of Christ? (I speak as a fool) I am more; in labours more abundant, in stripes above measure, in prisons more frequent, in deaths oft. . . . In weariness and painfulness, in watchings often, in hunger and thirst, in fastings often, in cold and nakedness." William Barclay, in his commentary on Corinthians (page 282), included fasting as Paul's "credential of an apostle." "For this reason I am sending to you Timothy, my son whom I love, who is faithful in the Lord. He will remind you of my way of life in Christ Jesus, which agrees with what I teach everywhere in every church" (1 Corinthians 4:17).

In Acts 13:3 the Holy Spirit "sent out" Paul and Barnabas. The great missionary church of Antioch, in Syria, was the physical entity equipped and chosen, then honored to participate. The greatness of that church lay not in who they were, but what they allowed the Holy Spirit to do through them. It was God's work. The fasting of Acts 13:2 was a vertical dimension. The diverse leadership of that church fasted "to" the Lord. This was personal introspection, laying oneself open to be searched and sent by the Lord.

The fasting of verse 3 was another area or role of fasting. In this case it was horizontal. Verse 2 exhibits reaching up to God, verse 3 shows reaching out to man. Vertical and horizontal meet at right angles. The Holy Spirit confirms a right angle of relationship, which includes God and reaching lost humanity with fasting as a catalyst in both.

From this [the Antiochian] church's officially sending out "foreign missionaries" we can learn many important principles about the missionary involvement of churches. How the church came to recognize this call of God is instructive. Tannehill [in *Narrative Unity*, page 161] shows how three features in this passage are found in two other Lukan commissioning passages: "The beginnings of the missions of Jesus and the apostles are preceded by references to prayer (Luke 3:21; Acts 1:14) and provide opportunity for action of the Spirit (Luke 2:5–41)." Prayer here is viewed as a service we do for God (Acts 13:2). To this is added fasting (13:3), which was also associated with the start of Jesus' ministry (Luke 4:2). Ralph Earle writes [in *Acts*, Carter and Earle, page 175] that fasting "emphasizes a state of uninterrupted concentration which made it possible to ascertain the will of the Lord. That is the main purpose and value of fasting."[7]

This is a remarkable instance of God's timing. Acts 13 and following passages mark the scene of Christianity moving from Jerusalem to Antioch, Syria. Christianity had its official beginning in Jerusalem under the cloud of Jewish culture. Peter, James and John were the principle leaders after Pentecost.

Under the leadership of the Holy Spirit, diverse prophets and elders, the church would henceforth be led by Gentile believers. The transfer to "divine service" was under the direction of the Holy Spirit, who said, "'I have called them.'"

The church was fasting when they were commanded to set apart Paul and Barnabas. The first formed mission to the Gentiles was an important event in the church. This endeavor was a new one and was filled with danger and hardships.[8] When direction from the Spirit was received, leaders in the church at Antioch fixed a day for the ordination and prepared for it by prayer and fasting. "While they were worshiping the Lord and fasting, the Holy Spirit said, 'Set apart for me Barnabas and Saul for the work to which I have called them.' So after they had fasted and prayed, they placed their hands on them and sent them off" (Acts 13:2, 3). With the departure of Barnabas and Saul, the second part of Acts begins.[9]

This first famous missionary tour had some features quite peculiar and is in some respects inimitable by us. But in other aspects it may be regarded as a typical work of God. It was begun by God (Acts 13:2–4). In his strength, it was carried out and completed. It was crowned by a recital to those by whom they represented. God opened the door of faith through which faithful men may enter.[10]

Andrew Murray, in his book, *Absolute Surrender*, affirms that fruit-bearing branches are dependent on the vine, avowing a direct relationship to churches on their knees with prayer and fasting. This accounts for the number of missionaries in the field. Our imperative from Jesus is to pray for reapers. The harvest is ripe; the laborers are few (Luke 10:2).

The first missionary journey led Paul and Barnabas to Cyprus and Asia Minor. Churches established along the way were Iconium, Lystra and Derbe. As the missionaries returned to Antioch to make a report, they revisited the newly established churches. Jewish leaders had developed the synagogue idea while in captivity and it seemed to carry over into the Jewish Christian communities. That became an issue we see from the action of the apostles whose duty it was to oversee the appointment of leaders. Paul and Barnabas revisited each congregation and appointed elders, "strengthening the disciples and encouraging them to remain true to the faith. 'We must go through many hardships to enter the kingdom of God,' they said. Paul and Barnabas appointed elders for them in each church and, with prayer and fasting, committed them to the Lord, in whom they had put their trust" (Acts 14:22, 23).

Paul and Barnabas were undoubtedly sent of God and were members of the church at Antioch. The church regarded them as representatives, followed them with sympathies, sustained them by prayers and received them back with warmest welcome—a most suitable crown to a noble work.[11]

Fasting in the New Testament seems to be connected to the belief in the imminence of Christ's return. The litany that accompanied the Eucharist, namely "Come Lord Jesus," reflected the urgency of *Parousia*. There seems to be less emphasis on each of these Christ-ordained disciplines the further removed from their establishment we are by time. The earliest Christians must have seen a value that contemporary Christians disregard. Obviously the dust of millennia has shrouded some of these realities. There is not a habit or weakness that can survive a siege of prayer and fasting. Prayer alone is just one half of the battle.[12]

What Jesus said about prayer and fasting must be emphasized, meaning it is not an occasional practice. It applies to all of us. It must be the culture, environment and the air we breathe that connects us with God to bring revival.

Revival for lost souls involves intimacy of spirit. Many religious and social programs exist to serve needs; however, evangelism/revival is not a program. It must be a power force enabled by the Holy Spirit—faith to faith, heart to heart. Souls are not statistics. They are living, eternal entities. They are not herded like cattle nor driven like machines. God created us one at a time, saves us one at a time, and will judge us one at a time.

The spirit of revival must reach masses, but people are saved one by one. Faithful intercession by those with calloused knees, storming heaven's throne room in prayer with fasting is the only way God has chosen to reclaim this fallen world. "The Father (God) said to the Son (*Logos*) Jesus, 'Ask me, and I will make the nations your inheritance, the ends of the earth your possession'" (Psalm 2:7, 8, paraphrase).

Current parachurch ministries have strategies for growth, but do not evangelize a lost world. Programs for organizing, motivating and encouraging people have their place for maintaining traditional liturgies. But in order for revival to sweep across our land as a brisk spring wind, more will be required than all the arsenals man can muster.

Pentecostal power was not generated by a human modus operandi. It came from an upper room where men and women with fresh visitation from a resurrected Jesus told them where to go and what to do: "Do not leave Jerusalem, but wait for the gift my Father promised, which you have heard me speak about. For John baptized with water but in a few days you will be baptized with the Holy Spirit" (Acts 1:4, 5).

The divine strategy included:

- Divine person (Jesus)
- Faithful intercessors (120 disciples)
- Place (divinely appointed)
- Divine results (multitudes saved)

It would be rather simplistic to tell you that prayer with fasting is the only criterion for revival. It is absolutely essential, but there is at least one additional prerequisite: Worshipping God with prayer and fasting for revival must be anointed.

It seems that this is God's way of connecting with the human spirit. In response to prayer, an anointing from God for revival is what the breath of life is to a human body crafted by the fingers of God from earthen soil. Nothing else in the universe looked like it. When the lifeless corpse of Adam received the breath of God, he was energized with life (Genesis 2:9).

In a similar way, God anointed Abraham's faith by the hand of his servant Melchizedek. The result was blessing beyond human comprehension. The oil that ran down Aaron's beard was a mere token of a larger invisible authority that the symbolic act represented. God anointed Abel's sacrifice by accepting it. Evidently God received Cain's sacrifice. Scripture says Cain's sacrifice to God was not accepted. Both gave something to God; he was in receipt of two sacrifices. However, Abel's sacrifice was anointed, received, approved, honored and desired. Cain's sacrifice did not receive God's approval. It was a dead issue; there was no life, no continuity to it. Abel's gift was so highly honored that millennia after his body had decayed "his faith yet speaks." The difference is in the anointing. God anointed the first fruits of harvest by accepting and blessing them. A symbolic act was performed when oil was poured over Saul's head and David's as well. What was the difference? David received a conscious connection to God; it seems to me that Saul did not.

So, prayer and fasting for revival must receive an anointing from God. People of God worship him with prayer and fasting, with a passion that will incite the corridors of heaven to dispatch a corps of angels to bring the Father's special anointing. With loud cries and tears, Jesus was heard (see Hebrews 5:7). Come, blessed Holy Spirit, pour out upon us now.

End Notes
Chapter 5—Fasting in the New Testament

1 John C. Wilhelmsson, "The Philosophical Contributions of Edith Stein" (academic thesis), San Jose State University, CA, 2016, 9.

2 George Robinson, *Isaiah, Pulpit Commentary* (Grand Rapids: Eerdmans, 1950), 373.

3 Aaron Milanec, *The Didache* (Collegeville, MN: Liturgical Press, 2003), 21.

4 Lyman Coleman, *Ancient Christianity* (London: Forgotten Books Ltd., 2015 [reprint of original ed. 1852]), 552.

5 Coleman, 554.

6 Coleman, 554, 555.

7 Stanley N. Gundry, *The NIV Application Commentary, Acts* (Grand Rapids: Zondervan, 1998), 376-377.

8 Albert Barnes, *Notes on the New Testament, Acts of the Apostles* (Grand Rapids: Baker, 1953), 198.

9 H.D.M. Spence, *The Pulpit Commentary, Acts and Romans*, Vol. 18 (Grand Rapids: Eerdmans, 1950), 401.

10 Spence, 412-413.

11 Spence, 411.

12 Edward Earle Purinton, *The Philosophy of Fasting* (New York: Benedict Lust Publisher, 1906).

CHAPTER 6

Alexander Campbell on the Subject of Fasting

━━

Alexander Campbell was editor of *The Millenial Harbinger,* 1832–1865. The following excerpts are from articles appearing in the periodical during the period 1832–1849 as follows:

- 1832 p. 188–191
- 1833 p. 515–522
- 1833 p. 568–573
- 1833 p. 601–604
- 1834 p. 106–107
- 1840 p. 160–166
- 1849 p. 255–257

Spelling and punctuation have been left as they appear in the original publication.

Query on Fasting—[*From Georgia.*] 1832
"Should Christians at any time attend to religious fasting?"

On this subject the Scriptures are plain, and, we think, very satisfactory. The Saviour taught his disciples in his Sermon on the Mount how they should demean themselves in their private fastings. Farther on in his history, in answer to some questions concerning the apparent neglect of fasts among his disciples, he informed them that although it would then be inconsistent for his disciples to fast under the present circumstances, according to the current views of fasting among the Jews, yet a time should come, after his departure from them, when fasts would be every way seasonable, consistent, and commendable.

We discover that fasting was frequent amongst the primitive disciples. As the brethren in Antioch ministered to the Lord and *fasted*, the Holy Spirit said, "Separate me Barnabas and Saul," &c. and when they had *fasted* and prayed, and laid their hands upon them, they commended them to the Lord. The church was fasting at the time this order was given. In the 14th chapter of the Acts, it reads, in the old English Bibles, 225 years ago, "And when they had ordained them elders by election in every church, and prayed and *fasted*, they commended them to the Lord in whom they believed." Even fasting in its full import, is spoken of by Paul, not only in reference to churches and individuals, but in reference to the connubial relation. 1 Corinthians 7:5. "That you may give yourselves to *fasting* and prayer." Thus fasting is alluded to in reference to the privacy of the closet, to the family relation, and to the whole congregation. So that not only did pious Jews, like Anna, "serve God with *fastings* and prayers," but so did the primitive Christians.

It was not positively enacted in the five books of Moses to the Jews; nor is it in the form of a positive command enjoined in the New Testament. Nor, indeed, could it so be, in reference to that delicate propriety which characterizes all the divine institutions; but it is so commended and enjoined by the examples of Jesus and Christians, and so *approbated by God*, as to leave no doubt that it contributes much to the *sanctification* of Christians to deny even their natural and necessary appetites occasionally, that they may glorify God with their bodies and spirits which are God's, be more spiritually-minded, and be more consecrated to the Lord. Concerning the utility and necessity of fasting, more hereafter.

Editor
From discussion around the dinner table in Campbell's home.

Mr. Williamson.—I acknowledge it is not improbable; but if on other occasions we are authoritatively informed that such a course was pursued by the tempter, it is not necessary that we should be always told the whole process of every temptation. It has just occurred to me, in corroboration of these remarks, that all God's ministers, whether angels or men, Prophets or Apostles, in executing their various errands with men, have addressed themselves to them by arguments. This being God's way in inclining and inducing men to action, it is not reasonable that he has also a secret and unintelligible way of addressing men's minds in order to give effect to the mode which he has uniformly pursued. Such a double method would only argue the impotency of all that is written in the book—of all the labors of prophets, apostles, and angels, in all their embassies to our race.

Mr. Reed.—It would be still more derogatory to the Spirit which spoke in all these messengers, if it were obliged to adopt a secret method to give efficacy to a public method. It would be making void the latter, and tacitly declaring it wholly inadequate to any good purpose: for without the labors of so many agents, it could have better done the work of persuasion by itself alone, and thus have saved the world from all the frauds which by a written revelation and by the ministry of angels and of men, have been practiced upon our race.

Robert Fowler.—Before you dismiss the subject, I must renew my difficulty touching the omnipresence of Satan. How can Satan instigate all the human race at one time to all the evil actions which are ascribed to him?

Mr. Reed.—Satan being the head, commander, and chief of all the evil agents in the universe, it is in strict harmony with universal usage to ascribe to him all that is done by his influence. For example, Cesar, while in Rome, was said to be transacting certain affairs in Germany, in Italy in Spain, in France, &c. Cesar was doing all these things by his agents; and, in the common sense of all the empire, everything was ascribed to him. Now as Satan has under him all evil spirits and wicked men, it is in full accordance with the same common sense of mankind, to ascribe to him all that is done by this influence. Thus Satan, like a roaring lion, is represented as going up and down in the earth, seeking whom he may devour.

Mrs. Reed.—Our Divine Master taught his disciples, in an early part of his ministry to pray, "Lead us not into temptation." Now methinks there is a necessity for us to watch and pray that we fall not into temptation.

Mrs. Fowler.—Let me add, sister Reed, that *fasting* still appears to me as a necessary accompaniment of watching and prayer. These three, each in its proper place and time, seem well adapted to our circumstances. We must *watch*, weigh, consider maturely the motives which govern our conduct. We must take heed lest Satan gain any advantage over us; keep our hearts with all diligence; and guard our tongues, which James says are sometimes "set on fire from hell," lest we offend our Lord. Watching is the constant duty in the time of war; while life lasts we are still exposed to the enemy, and therefore it is our duty always to watch. To pray is also necessary to our success. Jacob prevailed by prayer; while the hands of Moses were uplifted and upheld to the skies, Israel prevailed; when, by his side, Amalek prevailed. "Pray always" is an exhortation which shows its utility in waging the holy war. And why not *fast*? Does not the denial of our most reasonable appetites, the controlling of our lawful desires for food, accustom the mind to endure hardships, practice it in the most noble of all arts, that of self-government? It is easy for the mind, trained to govern the body in its most lawful desires to keep in subjection all inordinate appetites, to resist temptation; and pardon me if I yet express the conviction that the fasting of the Messiah, after his baptism and before his temptation, was designed as the best preparation for the labors he was about to commence, and the best protection and guard against the power of the enemy. It is of immense advantage to learn to keep the body under, in order to the elevation of our minds and affections to the heavens. This was not lost sight of by the great Apostle to the Gentiles. "I keep my body under," discloses the secret of his brilliant conquests in his career to glory. We pamper ourselves, and pray for humility and self-denial! Do you not think, Brother Reed, that this is inconsistent?

Mr. Reed.—I am convinced that the pampering and continued feasting of the body is a sin against nature and against religion. To fast when persons have no appetite to eat, or nothing to eat, is without moral advantage; but to deny our appetites when we have all the means of indulgence, and the keen desires of nature, in full health and vigor, is quite another matter, and has quite a different effect upon ourselves, especially when that fasting is designed to advance our conformity to the Lord. Thus fasting, our minds are more acute, our judgments less biased and oppressed by sense, our hearts better prepared for waiting upon the Lord, and our moral strength renewed and increased. I have not one word to say against fasting; but much to say in its favor.

Father Goodal.—A religion without fasting and the restraint of even our most natural and reasonable appetites, would not be adapted to our whole nature. Fasting is just as necessary to spiritual health as exercise is to our corporeal vigor. In all ages of the world, on all great occasions, seasons of sore trial, times of great calamity, public solemnities, the good and faithful and heavenly minded of our race gave themselves to fasting and prayer, as means of sanctification or preparation for the labors and trials that were coming upon them. My maxim on this subject, for the last forty years, has been that occasional fasting is good for both physical and moral health, and constant feasting or indulgence is good for neither. . . .

Mrs. Fowler.—It is not at all repugnant to my views of fasting, (and they are now fairly before the company,) that Christians should feast together from house to house, as well as fast, either publicly or privately, as occasion may require. Our blessed Saviour feasted as well as fasted; and I fully agree with Mother Goodal that there is a time for everything, and that all things are beautiful in their season.

Near Braddock's Grave, Oct. 7, 1833.
EDITOR
Fasting. No. 1
Introduction

"Beloved, now are we the children of God." How great the honor! How great our Heavenly Father's love towards us, that we should be called *children* of God! "For this reason," says the beloved disciple John, "the world does not know us, because it did not know him. However, we know that when he shall appear we shall be like him;—that we shall see him as he is. And every one who has this hope in him, purifies himself even as he is pure." How did we attain to this high relationship? By being born of God by water and Spirit. Having renounced the Prince of darkness with all human leaders, masters, and teachers in religion, and vowed allegiance to the King of kings, the Son of God, we are free indeed. It is no wonder, therefore, that we are hated, slandered, reproached, and vilified by the world—that all manner of evil is said against us falsely for the Lord's sake,—for the stand we have taken on his side in this adulterous age. 'However, we know'—the ancient disciples knew and we know—that when he, our great Captain shall appear, 'we shall be like him—that we shall see him as he is.' 'Having borne the image of the earthly, we shall also bear the image of the heavenly.' But how do we know it? Because our Lord has said, "The conqueror shall inherit all things." And Paul, "We are not of those who apostatize to perdition; but of those who persevere to the salvation of the soul." And why not? Because we have added, or are adding to our faith courage, and knowledge, and temperance, and patience, and godliness, and brotherly kindness, and love. We have done these things, or are doing them, because we have in us this hope—this glorious *hope* of the appearing of the great God, even of our Saviour Jesus Christ, and of being welcomed by him to those mansions he has now gone to prepare for them that love him. We know that he was holy, harmless, and undefiled and separate from sinners. Therefore, this is the character which we are perfecting in ourselves. We are not satisfied with having begun in the Spirit. We are pressing forward to the mark of Christian perfection. We are keeping our body under and bringing it into subjection. We are continually looking to Jesus the great leader and perfecter of the faith. We are learning of him, and striving after conformity to him in all things. In whatever circumstances placed, What would Christ answer? How would *he* conduct himself? are the questions; and these answered, we speak and act accordingly.—*Thus are we 'purifying ourselves, even as he is pure.'*

Christian brethren, are not these the principles by which we are, and wish to be, actuated in all things? I presume to answer for you. They are. But, high as is this our heavenly calling and relationship, it must be confessed that we have yet too much of the groveling character of servants: free as we have been made by the Son of God, the world is yet too much in our thoughts and affections: clear as are our apprehension and comprehension of some of the first principles of Christian doctrine, we still live in a dark and cloudy day—the most perfect of us have not yet unlearned all our sectarian errors, and we have much yet to learn as the disciples of Christ. *A neglected lesson follows—*

"Moreover, when you fast, look not dismal as the hypocrites, who disfigure their faces, that men may observe that they fast. Indeed, I say to you, they have their reward. But you, when you fast, anoint your head and wash your face, that your fasting may not appear to men, but to your Father; and your Father, to whom, though he is unseen himself, nothing is secret, will recompense you." Matthew vi.

Our great Teacher in this lesson evidently speaks of FASTING as a *duty.* He supposes *occasions* for it—he gives some directions about the *mode* of observing it—and he speaks of a *reward,* as consequent upon the *right performance* of it. Brethren, the subject on which we purpose to address a few short essays to you, is introduced. In our next we will endeavor to give a scriptural answer to the first question, which our lesson suggests.

Bethany, Va. Nov. 14th, 1833.
Fasting. No. 2

"Moreover, when you fast, look not dismal as the hypocrites, who disfigure their faces, that men may observe that they fast. Indeed I say to you, they have their reward. But you, when you fast, anoint your head and wash your face, that your fasting may not appear to men, but to your Father; and your Father, to whom, though he is unseen himself, nothing is secret, will recompense you." Matthew vi.

The first question, which our lesson suggests for consideration is, What is meant by *fasting*? What is the literal, obvious signification of the word—that which indicates the subject matter, and without which the *duty* (if fasting be a *duty*) is not attended to at all?

If now we were writing for *laymen*, we might refer for an answer to this question to the intelligent *clergy*—to all standard English dictionaries: but we write not for them: we write for the disciples of Christ, whose prayer continually is, *'Lord, what wilt thou have me to do?'* We *might* refer to the intelligent clergy and the dictionary; but this reference would be most unsafe on many words for them—on faith, repentance, baptism, for instance—on all that have been subjects of controversy. But we refer, Christians, directly to the Law and the Testimony—to the text and context of several passages in the Living Oracles, where the word *fasting* occurs.

1 Samuel ch. 12. It is written, "And David *fasted*, and went in and lay all night upon the earth. And the elders of his house arose and went to him to raise him up from the earth: but he would not, *neither did he eat bread with them.*" After this—"They set *bread* before him, *and he did eat.* Then said his servants unto him, What thing is this, that thou hast done? Thou didst *fast* and weep for the child while it was yet alive; but when the child was dead, thou didst arise *and eat bread.* And he said, While the child was yet alive, I *fasted* and wept." What can be more manifest than that David's fasting here spoken of, was *his not eating* bread? It was not his 'going in,' (wherever that might [be])—It was not his lying all night upon the earth—It was not his weeping.

Again: *Esther* iv. "The Esther bade them return Mordecai this answer. Go, gather together all the Jews that are present in Shushan, and *fast* ye for me"—How? We are informed in the very next words;—"*neither eat nor drink,* three days, night nor day: I also and my maidens will fast likewise; and now will I go in unto the king, which is not according to law: and if I perish, I perish. So Mordecai went his way, and did according to all that Esther had commanded him." Can any reader of this testimony—any *Christian* reader—persuade himself or herself to believe, that the fasting of Mordecai and the Jews with him, and of Esther and her maidens, here spoken of, consisted in anything else, than in *abstaining from food and drink?*—Or, whatever else they did or refrained from doing, that it did not, and could not, properly bear the name of *fasting*, if they had eat and drunk during this time as much as was usual for them at other times?... We presume not. What need, then, have we of further testimony? Is not the question answered, and the point established, that "*to fast*" means "to abstain from food;" and "*fasting*," "the abstaining from food." Most certainly, this was the literal obvious signification of the word in the passages we have considered from the Old Testament in the days of David and of Esther: and that it meant the same in New Testament times, one more passage from the Testimony of Matthew iv. will fully establish. "And after fasting forty days and forty nights, he was *hungry*. Then the tempter accosting him, said, If thou be God's Son, command that these stones become *loaves.* Jesus answering, said, It is written, Man lives not by *bread* only, but by everything which God is pleased to appoint." *Jesus fasted in abstaining from God.* "If fasting be a *duty*," we have said. A word or two now, under his head. In the passage last quoted, we are informed that *Jesus* fasted—that he connected fasting with prayer. If, now, *Jesus' praying* be an example for his followers; why not *his fasting* also? But more direct and explicit to this point—Matthew 18. A demoniac is brought to the disciples: but they could not cure him. Why not? Jesus answers: "This kind is not dispossessed unless by prayer and *fasting*; plainly implying, that had they fasted as well as prayed, which was equally a duty to be done, they might have been able to cure this kind of demoniacs also. Again: ix. Ch. "Then John's disciples addressing him, said, We and the Pharisees often fast; why do your disciples never fast? Jesus answered, Can the bridemen mourn while the bridegroom shall be taken from them, and then will they fast." Mark (2:18,19) and Luke (v.33–35) record the same question and answer—"They will fast." In other words, it shall be their *duty* to fast, and answer—they will perform it. To the same effect, the Saviour's instructions, first quoted in the conclusion of our last essay, and placed at the head of this—the lesson, which we are considering: "Moreover, *when you fast*," &c. Why thus introduce this subject? Why the directions which follow; "Look not dismal as the hypocrites *when you fast*," if fasting be not a duty? If you know these things, happy are you "if you do them."

ADELPHOS
Fasting. No. 3—Occasion, 1834

"To everything there is a season," said the wise man, "and a time for every purpose under the heaven." So it had been under the Patriarchal and Jewish dispensations; and so it was under the Christian. David fasted when afflicted by the sickness of his child—Esther, Mordecai, and the Jews with them fasted when threatened with destruction by the machinations of Haman; and the king and the people of Nineveh fasted immediately after Jonah the prophet had preached. "Yet forty days and Nineveh shall be overthrown." "For," says the testimony, "word came unto the king and he arose from his throne, and he laid his robe from him, and covered him with sackcloth and sat in ashes. And he caused it to be proclaimed and published through Nineveh (by the decree of the king and nobles,) saying, Let neither man nor beast, herd nor flock, taste anything; let them not feed nor drink water." Jonah iii. 6, 7. This is called (5th verse) 'the proclamation of a *fast*.' In these instances, and others which might be noticed, where we read in the Old Testament that individuals or a people fasted, we at once see there was *occasion* for it. So also in the New Testament. The Saviour spoke of occasions for fasting, saying, "The days will come when the bridegroom shall be taken away, then shall they (my disciples) fast;" and Luke, in the Acts of Apostles, speaks of their performance of this duty thus: "And as they were ministering to the Lord and fasting the Holy Spirit said, Separate to me Barnabas and Saul, for the work to which I have called them. And having fasted and prayed and laid hands on them they dismissed them." (xiii. ch.) "And Cornelius said, Four days ago I was fasting to this hour. (x. ch.) And Peter, it appears, was fasting and praying when the messengers from Cornelius arrived for him; and it is said he became "very hungry." But it is not necessary we presume to make other quotations to show that the Lord not only required fasting as a duty, but furnished occasions for it; and that these occasions were thus observed by these primitive disciples.

These occasions we have seen were, after the Lord was taken away from them—when they especially needed divine support and direction—when they were about to set apart by solemn ordination some of their number to particular fields of ministerial labor, in the Lord's harvest. And on all such and similar occasions, we here infer, that it is proper for the disciples of Christ to fast now.

Is anyone afflicted;—let him *fast* and *pray*. Is the state of vital religion low in any congregation—do its members forget their covenant obligations, and for weeks, and for months, absent themselves from its regular meetings, and from attendance upon its ordinances;—*then is there occasion for fasting*. Are there whisperings, backbiting and uncharitable suspicions indulged in, and evil insinuations thrown out by one member against another—Is that wholesome rule of discipline, given by the Saviour, Matt. Xviii. "If thy brother trespass against thee, go and tell him his fault between thee and him alone," wholly neglected;—*then is there occasion for fasting*. Is a congregation destitute of a settled pastor, bishop, or overseer; and would they have the Lord give them one—a man whom he would approve, and own and bless to their spiritual edification, and to the conviction and conversion of sinners;—*then there is occasion for fasting*. In fine,—Is a land or nation,—a town or country, visited, or threatened with a visit from famine, pestilence, or sword;— *then there is occasion for fasting*. CHOLERA has furnished,—is furnishing,—and probably will yet furnish, many occasions to Christians for fasting. O that they would more generally improve them in this manner, as they ought! "Who can tell," said the king and nobles of Nineveh, "if God will turn and repent, and turn away from his fierce anger that we perish not." And it is added, "God saw their works, that they turned from their evil way: and God repented of the evil that he had said that he would do unto them, and he did it not." Esther, Mordecai, and the Jews with them, *in this way*, had power with God and prevailed, and so did others, and so have others both in ancient and in modern times.

Fasting. No. 4. 1833-Modern Forms

"MOREOEVER, when you fast, look not dismal, as the hypocrites, who disfigure their faces, that men may observe that they fast. Indeed, I say to you, they have their reward. But you, when you fast, anoint your heads, and wash your face; that your fasting may not appear to men; and your Father, to whom, though he is unseen himself nothing is secret, will recompense you." Matthew vi. Some professed Christians tell us that the *mode* or *form* of an institution is nothing—only attend to the thing itself, it matters not *how*, and all is well. Others tell us, that the mode or form is everything; and the thing itself may therefore be neglected. They tell us that fasting is not what the word literally imports; but simply 'an abstaining from sin'—a washing of the face and an anointing of the head, that we appear not to men to fast.—That we may eat and drink as much as we please—that we need not deny ourselves any good thing,—only put on our Sunday clothes, and Sunday countenance, and go to meeting and hear a sermon; and then return and praise or blame the preacher, and keep on eating and drinking: and this is fasting. So liable are mankind to extremes! But, you will observe, my brethren, that the hypocrites are spoken of as *fasting*, as much as the disciples. They performed all as far as related to the subject matter: (that is, *that* in which fasting essentially consisted,) but they erred in the mode or form of it—in the adjuncts or circumstances. They fasted: but the disfiguring of their faces that they might appear to men to fast, was not acceptable to him who sees in secret: and so displeasing was it to him that the Saviour adds, "Indeed, I say to you, they have their reward."—That is, they have it as they go along in the reverences and praise of men. For their disregard to the *mode* or *form*, no reward is reserved for them to be conferred by your Father in heaven. Here observe, the sad or dismal countenance, the disfigured face, and the motive—that they might appear to men to fast, of the hypocrites; stand opposed to the anointing of the head, the washing of the face, and the motive—not to be seen of man, but of God, of the disciples of Christ. These adjuncts or circumstances we denominate the *mode* or *form* of fasting. Strictly and philosophically speaking, however, they are no more the *mode* or *form* of fasting, than is a mode or form of one of them—the real mode or form of a thing being inseparable from the thing itself. However, they are not altogether misnamed, if this name conveys the general meaning which is here intended by it. There is not, manifestly, that impropriety and absurdity in calling these adjuncts or circumstances, in a *figurative sense*, the mode or form of fasting, than there is in calling the subject matter of one thing, *primarily* and *literally*, the subject matter of another thing. . . . We are taught by the mode or form,—the adjuncts or circumstances, (or, whatever else you please to call them)—of fasting, brought to view in our lesson under consideration, what God does, and what he does not require of us in performing this duty. He does not require a disfigured face, and a sad countenance, and a deal of parade and show of humility. He does require the contrary: and with the contrary, he requires that preparation of heart, which will enable us to pray, and seek in earnest what we pray for. A preparation of *heart* is necessary to acceptable fasting. There must be integrity and sincerity in our souls—we must from the heart forgive everyone his brother his trespasses. If we have done wrong, we must feel willing to make reparation—to confess and forsake. In fine, we must feel willing to do, and *do it*, so far as we know, perfectly right. The Prophet Isaiah very strikingly confirms these remarks of ours in the 58th chapter of his prophecies: "Wherefore have we fasted, say they, and thou seest not? Wherefore have we afflicted our soul, and thou takest no knowledge? Behold in the day of your fast ye find pleasure, and exact all your labors. Behold ye fast for strife and debate, and to smite with the fist of wickedness. Ye shall not fast as ye do this day to make your voice to be heard on high. Is it such a fast that I have chosen—a day for a man to afflict his soul? Is it to bow down his head like a bulrush, and to spread sackcloth and ashes under him? Wilt thou call this a fast, and an acceptable day to the Lord? Is not this the fast that I have chosen? To loose the bands of wickedness, and to undo heavy burdens, and to let the oppressed go free, and that ye break every yoke? Is it not to deal thy bread to the hungry, and that thou bring the poor that are cast out to thy house? When thou seest the naked, that thou cover him, and that thou hide not thyself from thine own flesh."

The question has been asked, Is fasting a private, or a public, social duty? The scriptures we have already noticed answer this question. It is both. David, Cornelius and Peter fasted alone, in private; Esther and her maidens, Mordecai and the Jews with him, the king, the nobles, and the people of Nineveh—and the prophets and teachers of the church at Antioch fasted publicly. Fasting being connected with prayer is proper wherever and whenever prayer is proper.

ADELPHOS.
Fasting. No. 5--Reward. 1849

In our introductory article, under the above caption, dated, "*Bethany*, Nov. 14th, 1833," and published in volume IV, first series, of the Harbinger, we said:

"Our great Teacher, in this lesson, Matthew VI, speaks of **FASTING** as a *duty*. He supposes *occasions* for it,—he gives some directions about the *mode* of observing it,—and he speaks of a *reward* as consequence upon the *right performance* of it, p. 569.

In the three following papers,—published, No. 2, in the same volume, pp. 601—3, and Nos. 3 and 4, in volume V, of the same series, pp. 106—9, this duty was defined, explained and established. Something was also said of the *occasions* and *mode* of observing it. It remained then, and it has remained ever since, to say what is to be said of the reward of fasting.

Fifteen years have passed away, and with them how many—Oh, how many thousands, tens of thousands, and millions of our race! At least five hundred millions. How many of the disciples of Christ! How many, who, in 1833 and 1834, read these volumes with delight!—Some scores—perhaps fifties and hundreds of these are now numbered with the dead. Three of the nine children of "the excellent Olympas," within the last nine years, we are told, have died; three have married and left the paternal roof; and only the youngest three—Susan, James, and Henry, now remain at home! But father Olympas, and mother Julia, and six of their children, thank the Lord, and old father Goodal, too, and brothers Ephraim and Clement and Robert, and many others, still survive. The Lord having spared Adelphos, also, he would now offer for the acceptance of the brethren what follows on the "*Reward.*"

"*And your Father will recompense you,*" says the Master. And how? I answer—in body, soul and spirit.

It is the unanimous decision of the medical profession, that occasional fasting is most conducive to health; and many there are who, when at all indisposed, are accustomed to fast instead of taking medicine. And they are *cured* by it, they say. Does not this reveal the secret of the wonderful success of Homeopathists?

But it is with fasting, as a religious duty, with its mode or form, its adjuncts or concomitants as enjoined in the Book of God—to give spiritual health to the soul, that I would now speak of it. It is because it is so enjoined, that it has spiritual health in it; and for this, because our Father has connected—indissolubly connected—our duty and happiness, and even blesses his obedient children, and ever will bless all in fasting as he requires. In the performance of this duty he has promised to bless us. And how?

We turn, for the answer, to the Prophet Isaiah, 58th chapter, 8-12 verses.

> "Then shall thy light break forth as the morning, and thy health shall spring forth speedily."

Spiritual light and health, this! And it shall not wait; it shall be conferred at once; and darkness and sickness shall flee before them. "And thy righteousness shall go before thee."

You shall have a character, for being what you profess, that shall be known and read of all.—It shall be known, and by everyone acknowledged.

"The glory of the Lord shall be thy re-reward." What a backing up is this! And this is not all. No: you are now but just prepared for all the good things which God has in store for you. You have now got into that place and occupy that position where you may enjoy, and will enjoy, if you remain in it, a focal blaze of the Divine glory. "Then shall thou call and the Lord shall answer; then shalt thou cry, and he shall say, here I am."

Here you can pray and your prayers shall be heard. The Lord, by the Prophet, continues--"If thou take away from the midst of thee the yoke, the putting forth of the finger and speaking vanity; and if thou draw out thy soul to the hungry, and satisfy the hungry soul, then shall thy light rise in obscurity, and thy darkness be as the noon-day:

"If the light that is in thee be darkness," said our Lord, "how great the darkness!" But if the "darkness be as the noon-day," we ask how great shall be thy light! And this is not all. No: for he continues—

"And the Lord shall guide thee continually, and satisfy thy soul in drought, and make fat thy bones; and thou shalt be like a watered garden, and like a spring of water, whose waters fail not."

How rich and abundant these blessings! And what a variety! But more still—thou shalt not only be blest thyself, but thou shalt be a blessing to others:

"And *they that shall be* of thee shall build the old waste places; thou shalt raise up the foundations of many generations, and thou shalt be called the repairer of the breach, the restorer of paths to dwell in."

These—all these things enter into the "recompense," and God has promised and will confer them as a *reward* upon all his obedient children, who rightly perform the duty of fasting.

Brethren, do you know these things? Happy are ye if you practice them. Sturbridge, Mass., March 9, 1849.

Many of these biblical texts are found in *The Living Oracles: The New Testament Translated from the Original Greek* by Doctors George Campbell, James McKnight and Philip Doddridge, with an appendix by Alexander Campbell. Reprinted by Gospel Advocate Company, Nashville, TN, 1954.

"Alexander Campbell on the Subject of Fasting," excerpts from *The Millennial Harbinger*, complied by Daniel I. McWhirter and published by College Press Pub. Co., Joplin, MO, 1981.

CHAPTER 7

Questions and Answers on Fasting

This chapter includes material from a college classroom of which I was the instructor. The curriculum identified the course as a study on prayer. The class began with the following prayer:

Father, thank you for the opportunity to study this vital subject. Our prayers continue that you will cause us to develop into the kind of prayer warriors who will alter history. Forgive our transgressions, our sins, as we confess them in deep penitence and concern. In Jesus' name, Amen.

This morning we are answering questions on a subject that is unique to our ears: fasting. We have no biblical record of fasting prior to Moses. There may have been some self-imposed fasts for other reasons; however, for religious purposes we find no earlier reference.

QUESTION: *In the fast, after getting past the second day and feeling no hunger, how does one cope with the weakness?*

I do not know in your case, but in mine, I go through stages. There are levels of reserves of energy in the human body. Incidentally that is why fasting is good. Even if there were no after life, our system needs time to purge itself. What would happen to our city water system if they never did turn it off and back flush it? You'd get the pipes stopped up and that happens in our digestive system. A medical doctor who supports fasting told me that many hospitals impede the progress of healing because patients are over-fed when the body could be using its stored energy to support healing.

QUESTION: *In longer fasts you mentioned that one can take fluid. Are you talking about water or fruit juices?*

A rabbi with whom I studied, told the class that the biblical fast included wine. The two medical doctors with whom I conversed said the human body cannot live forty days without water. However, one can survive without food for several days. In Moses' situation, he was supernaturally sustained. The doctors also said that occasionally they impose fasting on a patient in the hospital. We are over-fed and over-stuffed in this country and as a result our organs are suffering.

QUESTION: *During a three-day or five-day fast, what kind of activity do you perform?*

A regular schedule. During a conference in Oklahoma many were fasting from Monday night until Thursday night. Thursday night a lady told me she left Monday night, thinking that idea was crazy. "I thought you had lost your mind. My body craves food," she said. "I couldn't handle it."

On Wednesday night, she came to me and said, "You know, I took the dare." I have never seen a person in a greater state of euphoria than she was that night. She said, "I have made it. I didn't believe I could. However, if other people could do it, I could," she said. So she took the dare, further stating, "I will frequently do this for the rest of my life. I cannot tell you the state of mind I am in right now with my Lord."

One must give up the lesser for the greater. It would be better if we took care of fasting privately as it is a highly personal matter. The disciples said, "Master, teach us to pray." Prayer and fasting are connected to Kingdom teaching by Jesus.

QUESTION: *Do you find any evidence in the Scriptures of fasting that the early church practiced?*

Yes, they often fasted; see, for example, Acts 13:2–3. Two corporate instances of fasting occurred here. In verse 2, the leadership of the church in Antioch fasted. This was vertical, reaching up to God. Verse 3 is an additional expression of fasting and prayer as Saul and Barnabas were sent on the first missionary journey. This was horizontal, reaching out to man. Prayer and fasting was the centerpiece of that ministry.

QUESTION: *When adding shepherds or other church leaders, should the whole congregation participate in fasting as a group?*

Yes. Notice Acts 14:21–23:

They preached the good news in that city and won a large number of disciples. Then they returned to Lystra, Iconium and Antioch, strengthening the disciples and encouraging them to remain true to the faith. We must go through many hardships to enter the kingdom of God, they said. Paul and Barnabas appointed elders for them in each church and, with prayer and fasting, committed them to the Lord, in whom they had put their trust.

QUESTION: *What is the minimum fast?*

When fasting for the first time, start with a meal or two. Gradually add longer periods such as a twenty-four hour period.

For additional questions and answers on fasting, I recommend Arthur Wallis's book, *God's Chosen Fast: A Spiritual and Practical Guide to Fasting* (Fort Washington, PA: CLC Publications, 1968), 142–149. Also Jerry Falwell and Elmer Towns, *Fasting Can Change Your Life* (Ventura, CA: Regal Books, 1998), 251–273.

Additional Reasons to Fast

1. Fasting for greater focus on God.
   - Jesus, full of the Holy Spirit (Luke 4:1–2).
   - To seek God as your life source (Luke 4:4).
   - To seek God in worship and service (Luke 4:8).

2. Fasting for direction and purpose.
   - "While they were worshiping the Lord and fasting, the Holy Spirit said . . ." (Acts 13:2).
   - Seeking wisdom from above (Proverbs 1:8–9).
   - Seeking spiritual advice (Acts 9:9).

3. Fasting to battle evil.
   - Loosen the chains of evil (Isaiah 58:6).
   - Subduing wickedness in Jesus' name (Matthew 17:19–20).
   - With prayer and fasting "no weapon (of evil) forged against you will prevail" (Isaiah 54:17).

4. Fasting for victory.
   - "So we fasted . . . and he [God] answered our prayer" (Ezra 8:23)
   - Seeking God in problem solution (John 14:13, 14).
   - When suffering for the sake of the gospel (2 Timothy 1:12).

5. Fasting to display the image of God (2 Corinthians 3:18).
   - That the beauty of Jesus may be reflected: ". . . then your righteousness shall go before you" (Isaiah 58:8).
   - To become fruit bearing disciples (John 15:7–8, 16).

6. Fasting for divine health.
   - "And your healing will quickly appear" (Isaiah 58:8).
   - That the Holy Spirit may renew the mind and give mental strength (Romans 12:2; Philippians 2:5, 4:4–7).

7. Fasting for personal holiness.
   - "Blessed are the pure in heart" (Matthew 5:8).
   - To share in His holiness (Hebrews 12:10).

- Holiness allows one to see the Lord (Hebrews 12:14).

8. Fasting for greater faith, freedom and protection. "Have faith in God and you will be upheld; have faith in his prophets and you will be successful" (2 Chronicles 20:20).
   - Jehovah receives a sincere fast.
   - "The Lord is my helper; I will not be afraid" (Hebrews 13:6).
   - "So if the Son sets you free, you will be free indeed" (John 8:36).
   - The full armor of God (Ephesians 6:10–18).

9. Fasting for the compassion of Jesus.
   - "When Jesus saw the large crowd, he had compassion on them and healed their sick" (Matthew 14:14).
   - "The true fast is to share your food with the hungry and provide shelter for the poor wanderer" (Isaiah 58:7).
   - Attention and care for those in need will allow the King to reply, "I tell you the truth, whatever you did for one of the least of these brothers of mine, you did it for me" (Matthew 25:40).

10. Fasting for intimacy with God.
    - Moses fasted forty days in the presence of God (Exodus 34:28).
    - Elijah fasted forty days on his way to Horeb (1 Kings 19:8).
    - Jesus fasted forty days in the wilderness (Matthew 4:1-2).
    - While no one can affirm that fasting accounts for a supreme level of intimacy with God, neither should it be neglected as unimportant. The Lord embraced it. It is interesting to note that for the last 2000 years the names of Christian leaders who prayed and fasted have not disappeared. "This is the victory that has overcome the world, even our faith. Who is it that overcomes the world? Only he who believes that Jesus is the Son of God" (1 John 5:4-5).

11. Fasting during national crisis (2 Samuel 1:12).

12. Fasting with evil intent (Acts 23:12-13).

Adapted from *Prayer and Fasting*, Prayer Point Press.

Physical Aspects of Fasting

When practiced with due care and sense, fasting is beneficial to the physical body. Here are some points to observe if you wish to obtain the physical benefits of fasting:

1. Always remember "your body is the temple of the Holy Spirit" (1 Corinthians 6:19). It pleases God when you take proper care of your body, seeking to make it a clean and healthy temple.

2. If you are on a regular medication, or suffer from heart, circulatory or diabetic diseases, it is wise to obtain medical advice before entering into any fast that extends beyond a meal or two.
3. In the early period of a fast, you may experience unpleasant symptoms, such as dizziness, headache, nausea, etc. Usually, these are indications that your fasting is overdue and that you need the purifying physical action of fasting in various areas of your body.
4. Remember that hunger is partly a matter of habit. In the early stages of a fast, hunger will probably return at each normal mealtime. But if you hold out, missing a few meals will not create permanent injury.
5. During a fast, some people drink only water. Others drink various kinds of liquids, such as fruit juices, broth or skim milk. Work out for yourself the particular pattern of fasting that suits you best as an individual. It is wise to abstain from strong stimulants such as tea and coffee.
6. It is scriptural to abstain at times from fluids as well as from solid foods. However, do not exceed seventy-two hours. This was the limit set by Esther and her maidens (Esther 4:16).
7. Break a fast gradually. Begin with foods that are easy to digest. The longer the fast, the more careful one will need to be when breaking the fast.

Guidelines for Individual Fasting

1. Enter into fasting with positive faith.
2. Remember that "faith cometh by hearing and hearing by the word of God" (Romans 10:17). Fasting should be based upon the conviction that God's Word enjoins this as a part of normal Christian discipline (Matthew 6:16–18).
3. Do not wait for some emergency to drive you to fasting. It is better to begin fasting when you are spiritually "up" rather than when you are "down." The path of progress in God's kingdom is "from strength to strength" (Psalms 84:7).
4. Do not set too long a period of fasting to begin. If you are fasting for the first time, begin by omitting one or two meals. Then move on gradually to longer periods, such as a day or two days. It is better to begin by setting a short period as your objective, and achieve it. If you set too long a period to begin, and fail to achieve it, you will become discouraged and give up all together.
5. During your fast, give plenty of time to Bible reading. Where possible, read a portion of Scripture before each period of prayer.
6. It is often helpful to set certain specific objectives in your fasting and to make a written list of these.

7. Avoid religious ostentation and boastfulness (Matthew 6:16).
8. Keep a check on your motives each time you fast. Do not vow to God without strong intentions of keeping your vow.

Guidelines for Collective Fasting

For periods of collective public fasting, all the guidelines given above for individual fasting will normally continue to apply. In addition, here are a few special points to observe in connection with collective fasting:

1. In Matthew 18:19, Jesus emphasizes the special power that exists when believers "agree" together in prayer. To this end, all those participating in a collective fast should do everything in their power to achieve and maintain agreement with each other.
2. People participating in a collective fast should make a commitment to pray specifically for each other during the period of the fast (Acts 14:23).
3. A meeting place should be chosen where those participating in the fast can come together, at times mutually agreed upon, for prayer and exhortation.

Adapted from Derek Prince, *Shaping History Through Prayer and Fasting* (Old Tappan, NJ: Revell, 1973), 114–117.

CHAPTER 8

Fasting, The Integration of Mind and Heart

Of all of God's creation, mankind is unique. Even the angels, created beings of the celestial realm, did not have bodies of flesh with which to contend. Man is physical-carnal and earthy; man is spiritual-sacred and eternal. How does one mix water and oil?

Philosophy and theology are essentially a transcript and an interpretation of human experiences which involves warfare in the human soul. To Paul that was warfare between two opposing forces that he called the flesh and the spirit. "The desires of the flesh are against the spirit," he said, "and the desires of the spirit are against the flesh, for these are opposed to each other" (Galatians 5:17). "I delight in the law of God in my inmost self," he says, "but I see in my members another law at war with the law of my mind" (Romans 7:22). Here for Paul was the dilemma of the human situation.[1]

Fasting is abstaining from food and/or other good things, in order to achieve or obtain something better. It is not wrong to eat, drink, sleep, work, etc. When Jesus was hungry, he ate. When Jesus was thirsty, he drank. When weary, he rested and/or slept. That is in order. We are human, physical.

But man also has a spiritual capacity. The biblical description of man is a spirit with a mind who lives in a body (1 Thessalonians 5:23). The greater part of man is his immortality. The physical is temporary at best. The Christian must not be solely governed by the physical part of himself. Infinite *nephesh* (soul) is spiritual. It may be led and governed by the Holy Spirit.

Fasting gives additional weight to prayer. When we begin to fast and pray, it means that we have settled down to the real business of praying with persistence. It is certain that God's people would see more answers to their prayers, if they would miss more meals and spend that time in prayer.

In early church history, fasting was considered one of the pillars of the Christian religion. When the church had power, fasting was an essential part of the faith. But today, fasting is a lost art, little practiced and rarely taught. Fasting is not mere abstinence from food or from any other pleasure, in itself. Rather it is abstinence with a purpose.

Fasting reveals that one has come to the place of spiritual desperation. It means that you are now determined at all costs to put God first. There are times when we should turn our backs on everything in the world, even our daily food, in seeking the face of God. Fasting means that we are determined to seek the face of God and get our prayers answered. It means that we put God first, before everything, including food.

Ordinarily, fasting means to abstain from food, but the same spirit of desperation will also lead us to abstain from other things as well. The authentic battle is between the flesh and the spirit. Fasting is a voluntary disuse of anything innocent in itself, with a view to spiritual culture. It does not necessarily apply to food only. It applies to everything that the natural man may desire. So fasting involves putting God first when one prays, wanting God more than one wants food, more than sleep, more than one wants fellowship with others, more than one wants to attend to business. How could a Christian ever know that God was first in his life if he did not at times turn from every other duty and pleasure to give himself wholly to the seeking of the Face of God?

The great lack of our life is that we do not pray and fast more. Prayer moves the Hand that moves the universe, and fasting adds weight to prayer. It secures for the believer the resources of divinity.[2]

Working in the invisible or unseen realm is the highest possible form of mental and spiritual activity. This is done by prayer and fasting. It is one thing to give your time, money, and talent. It is quite another thing to voluntarily abstain from food, subjecting the physical in the interest of promoting the spiritual. This, at least, is utilizing the "heavenly nature."

As faith is stronger than fear, as God is stronger than Satan, so the spiritual is stronger than the physical part of man. Fasting, connected with the prayer of faith, is a means by which the spiritual integrates with the physical to make a person God's person. It is the judgment of this author that when one subjects the physical in the interest of the spiritual, there is a special act of God to convert power to the human heart that is not to be had otherwise. I do not say this was the exclusive idea in Paul's mind, but I firmly contend it was included when he said, "I buffet my body." I voluntarily subject the physical in the interest of promoting the spiritual. Fasting fits into this development. Pray and meditate and grow in this grace.

I am not impressed with the teaching that my body can do one thing and my spiritual part essentially another. The biblical teaching on fasting as rightfully understood and employed, posits the opposite—namely, that while I am flesh or physical, there is also a divine part of me. These two unlike elements brought together by the divine Creator may be more tranquil in "my human situation" than is often the case.

A principle issue in the integration of mind, heart or spirit is faith. This is where authentic faith becomes important. A mature faith requires a believer to move from the logical, rational and intuitive mental stage to a level of trust in God beyond the physical level. Mark 11:22 states in the Greek text "to have God's faith, or have the faith of God."[3] Human, logical "faith" caused Thomas to deny the report of ten apostles that Jesus was resurrected (John 20:25). Often I ask, "which is greater, God's faith in man or man's faith in God?" John Chrysostom (347–407 AD), a bishop, said, "Fasting gives power to our prayer." How? It interferes with the natural and promotes the spiritual. No well-known revival since Pentecost existed without prayer and fasting. The mind is the repository of information. Based upon biblical truth the Holy Spirit utilizes that information and brings transformation in the heart or spirit of man. A classic illustration of prayer and faith is George Müller of Bristol, England (1805–1898). Consider these words from his tract, *How to Ascertain the Will of God*:

1. I seek at the beginning to get my heart into such a state that it has no will of its own in regard to a given matter. Nine-tenths of the difficulties are overcome when our hearts are ready to do the Lord's will, whatever it may be. When one is truly in this state, it is usually but a little way to the knowledge of his will.
2. Having done this, I do not leave the result to feelings or simple impression. If so, I make myself liable to great delusions.
3. I seek the will of the Spirit of God through, or in connection with, the Word of God. The Spirit and the Word must be combined. If I look to the Spirit alone without the Word, I lay myself open to great delusions also. If the Holy Ghost guides us at all, he will do it according to the Scriptures and never contrary to them.
4. Next I take into account providential circumstances. These often plainly indicate God's will in connection with his Word and Spirit.
5. I ask God in prayer to reveal his will to me aright.
6. Thus through prayer, the study of the Word and reflection, I come to a deliberate judgment according to the best of my ability and knowledge, and if my mind is thus at peace, and continues so after two or three more petitions, I proceed accordingly. In trivial matters, and in transactions involving most important issues, I have found this method always effective.

H.T. Hamblin wrote in his book, *A Venture of Faith*, that George Müller sustained and maintained his faith through prayer. On a trip to Bristol, an offer was given to me by the curator of the museum to examine the writings of Mr. Müller. His study Bible through which he prayed more than one hundred times had many notations regarding prayer and fasting. His statements were very challenging. Certainly, the invisible is the cause of outward happenings.

Godly prayer with fasting and persevering faith ennobles communication with God. Such prayer is not a mere asking for things, but is a seeking for God until he is found. Then we know all is well.[4] Prayer not only maintains our faith, it also brings us into a relationship with God who makes all things possible.

The blessings that have been granted to prayer and fasting illustrate its importance and worth. The records of religious history prove that God is the hearer of prayer, both that of great magnitude and also of those prayers of lesser moment.

In assessing the prayer life, faith and work of George Müller, it becomes clear that a major principle which undergirded his life was the relationship between prayer and faith. A natural consequence of his ministry always extolled God as a giver. This laid the foundation stone of the invisible kingdom of God on earth.[5]

These inseparable principles sustained and maintained him throughout his ministry from 1830 until his death in 1898. His greatest achievements and victories were won in his study because it was there that he spent hours and hours reading his Bible and praying. It was an honor for me to visit Bristol and his study, to sit in his chair behind his desk and to hold his Bible.

In prayer he poured out his heart to God, telling him everything. As he read the Scriptures he found God speaking to him. This is safer than listening to distant, faint voices or whatever is thought to be the voice of God. Thoughts and ideas from Scripture become alive as the Holy Spirit gives one what is needed in such an hour.

Those who study the life of George Müller, although he would probably be embarrassed by such attention, stand in awe of this true pioneer's dependence on God expressed through his prayer and faith. He once said, "all our need is my comfort." He trusted in the living God for everything.[6] Perhaps his faith in God was on a par with, or even exceeded, that of any one of the twelve apostles. He was given a unique gift from God. His special gift was not the first of its kind. However, it allows us to see that mortals from Noah until now have been few in whom God could trust as he did George Müller. Müller found a new and better way to live.

What was that, you may ask? His way was not to acquire, possess, hold, defend or fight for this earth's wealth, but letting go. He depended on the divine, the unseen (invisible) realm, instead of his own efforts or worldly standards. Man cannot control the visible. After much prayer, George Müller embarked upon a daring adventure. The plight of orphans in England during this time was deplorable. He confronted the challenge in the following way: "Now, if I, a poor man, simply by prayer and faith, obtained without asking any individual the means for establishing and carrying on an Orphan House, there would be something which with the Lord's blessing might be instrumental in strengthening the faith of the children of God. It would also be a testimony to the conscience of the unconverted, of the reality of the things of God."[7] Many were the nights when Mary Müller would miss her husband and find him on his knees agonizing over lost souls, neglected children or God's will for a particular decision. He often prayed all night in order to reach "the sense of certainty."

There was a period of time from 1840 to the 1850s (I call these the "lean years") when Müller's work appeared to suffer. This deeply impacted and tried his soul. He was no god or super-human, and he admitted anxiety. He said his was "an ordinary faith, full of weaknesses." He admitted to times of doubt and fear. However, he continued to wait for God's direction and overcame his anxieties through prayer, rather than cave in and give up. He continued to pray and fast and wait on God until he knew once again that "all is well," and it always is, because the God of Elijah can never fail.

On October 21, 1868, he entered this in his diary, "As the days come, we make known our requests to him, for our outgoings have now been for several years at the rate of more than one hundred pounds each day; but though the expenses have been so great, *he has never failed us.*"

Year by year the increase of needs followed by God graciously supplying them is noted in his journal. Writing on July 28, 1874, he says,

It had for months appeared to me, as if the Lord meant . . . to bring us back to the state of things in which we were for more than ten years, from August 1838 until April, 1849, when we had day by day, almost without interruption, to look to him for our daily supplies, and for a great part of the time, from meal to meal. The difficulties appeared to me indeed very great, as the Institution is now twenty times larger than it was then and our purchases are to be made in a wholesale way; but I am comforted by the knowledge that God is aware of all this. The funds were thus expended; but God, our infinitely rich Treasurer, remains to us. It is this which gives me peace. Moreover if it pleases him, with a work requiring about 200,000 pounds a year, to make me do again at the evening of my life, what I did from August 1838 to April 1849, I am not only prepared for it, but gladly again I would pass through all these trials of faith if he only might be glorified and his church and the world be benefited.

Often this last point has of late passed through my mind and I have placed myself in the position of having no means at all left, and two thousand and one hundred persons not only daily at the table, but with everything else to be provided for and all funds gone; 189 missionaries to be assisted, and nothing whatever left; about one hundred schools, with about nine thousand scholars in them, to be entirely supported and no means for them in hand; about four millions of tracts and tens of thousands of copies of the Holy Scriptures yearly now to be sent out, and all the money expended.

Invariably, however . . . I have said to myself: "God, Who raised up this work through me, God, Who has led me generally year after year to enlarge it, God, Who has supported this work now for more than forty years, will still help . . . and He will provide me with what I need in the future also."[8]

Ole Hallesby, in his classic book, *Prayer*, shares this thought:

The secret prayer chamber is a bloody battleground. Here violent and decisive battles are fought out. Here the fate of souls for time and eternity is determined, in quietude and solitude, without another soul as spectator or listener . . .

Prayer has one function, and that is to answer "Yes," when he knocks, to open the soul and give him the opportunity to bring us the answer.

This throws light on the struggles and strivings, the work and the fasting connected with prayer. All these things have but one purpose: to induce us to open our hearts and to receive all that Jesus is willing to give, to put away all those things which would distract us and prevent us from hearing Jesus knock, that is, from hearing the Spirit of prayer when he tries to tell us what God is waiting to give us if we will only ask for it.

However, Hebrews 11:3 says that in the invisible realm, the realm beyond human sight, we find the real cause of all that manifests itself in this physical, visible world. In no way did Abraham, Paul or George Müller just let it slide and hope for the best. Absolutely not!

A different kind of prayer is to approach the Spiritual, the Eternal and pray that the will of the Holy God be done in my life. The prayer of faith believes it has already come to pass. In Genesis 18:10 the *Logos*, the Lord, said to Abram, "this time next year your wife, Sarah, will have a son." Romans 4:17 says Abraham believed in a God who calls things that are not as if they already were. John 8:56 records the startling statement that Abraham saw Jesus. He believed God.

Abraham was permitted to have a view of the death of the Messiah as a sacrifice for sin, represented by the command to offer Isaac (Genesis 22:1-13). Well might the eyes of a patriarch rejoice to be permitted to look in any manner on the sublime and glorious scene of the Son of God dying for the sins of men. Jesus said that he existed before Abraham. John 8:58 affirms that while he was a man, he was also endowed with another nature existing before Abraham.[9]

Living and working in the invisible is the highest form of mental and spiritual activity. To achieve by means of the "spirit" or "invisible" is not easy. It is not for the faithless, weak, timid or cowardly heart. It is a great achievement and no great feat is easy. This way of life requires a continual waiting on God. One does not fear or doubt—uncertainty must be overcome. A sense of God's presence and provision is nurtured through prayer and fasting. In such a faith circumstance Abraham's arm was caught in mid-air by the voice of an angel. Caught by the horns in a thicket was a ram placed there by an unseen God, and Abraham shouted, "Jehovah-Jirah, Jehovah-Jirah," God will provide—and God will never, never ask you to made a sacrifice for which he does not make the provision—provided you have the courage to walk with him into the water, no matter how deep or wide.

This life necessitates a continual waiting (in patience) upon God. This must never cease. This is the way that all fear, doubt, and uncertainty are overcome. One will then have a sense of understanding. Then you will know intuitively, through the work of the Holy Spirit. One author called this "soul-knowing"—the certainty that all is well, now and forever.

It is faith in extremity, when one realizes that a Sovereign God is in control—at that point one may become centralized in truth. Eternalized! We become anchored to the unchanging and eternal. We become established in the divine order.

There are different kinds of prayer. Some contemporary theologians have taught that positive mental attitudes and opulent psychological posturing account for prayer. That kind never gets beyond the stars. While some progress may be recorded, it is not prevailing prayer. We must comprehend the absolute basic to remain within the will of God. To fail will only prolong man's suffering.

The selfish or self-willed seeks only a physical good. What the finite mind thinks is good, may indeed be good. But prayer to the Eternal and Highest is for the larger good—often eternal and unseen. This must be in harmony with the highest will and purpose of heaven.

We are both invited and commanded to pray—it is for our highest good. This quality is the only one that can truly satisfy, make us happy and fill us with joy permanently and eternally. This is God's law concerning prayer. George Müller did not pray first for the orphanages, missionaries or materials. Rather, he prayed that the will of God be done, and done to the Glory of God. He prayed for specific, detailed, trivial, small matters, because it was clear in his mind that it was all about God.

If we do not pray, we cannot expect to receive. If, according to James, the brother of Jesus, we pray in our own self-will, we receive not because "we ask amiss." That means it is not in harmony with God's will. On the other hand, as one prays according to the will of God and does not receive that for which he prayed, it usually means that God has something else, more or better, than what was asked. For example, consider Mary and Martha in John 11 and Mary and the gardener in John 19.

God wants to give us his best, but we must ask for it. We must believe for it in the unseen realm. Through faith we make contact with the source of good, in order that the best will be manifested in the physical realm.

We must maintain the healthy exercise of our faith through faithful praying. This will maintain, renew and refresh our inner man. This cannot happen without the gift of the God-kind of faith. Prayer is not really asking God and receiving things, but rather seeking for and reaching after God until we find him, realizing that God is God and all is well, and that we have entered into liberty indeed. Our Christian life is perfected as it is imaged in the mind of God. The prayer of faith brings our mind into harmony (*cosmos*) with the sovereign will of God. This brings a quality of spirit into reality in our earthly walk.

> "For my thoughts are not your thoughts,
>   neither are your ways my ways,"
>   declares the LORD.
> "As the heavens are higher than the earth,
>   so are my ways higher than your ways
>   and my thoughts than your thoughts.
> As the rain and the snow
>   come down from heaven,
> and do not return to it
>   without watering the earth
> and making it bud and flourish,
>   so that it yields seed for the sower and bread for the eater,
> so is my word that goes out from my mouth:
>   It will not return to me empty,
> but will accomplish what I desire
>   and achieve the purpose for which I sent it."
> (Isaiah 55:8–11)

The same principle God used in the natural realm he used in the realm of the Spirit. The rain waters the earth and makes it flourish. God has reason or purpose for what he does in both the spiritual and the natural realm. The word of the Lord places his thoughts in our thoughts. That is information. This accounts for the rain which gives life to the earth. The Holy Spirit awakens the word of God in our hearts and by prayer and fasting quickens it into transformation of life. The result of rain and snow produce fruit. The fruit of the Spirit in a human is expressed in a beautiful metaphor found in Isaiah 55:11, 13: "So is my word that goes out from my mouth: It will not return to me empty, but will accomplish what I desire and achieve the purpose for which I sent it. . . . This will be for the LORD's renown, for an everlasting sign, which will not be destroyed."

END NOTES
Chapter 8 - The Integration of Mind and Spirit

1 William Barkley, *Flesh and Spirit*, (Grand Rapids: Baker, 1962), 9.

2 Gordon Cove, *Revival Now Through Prayer and Fasting* (Salem, OH: Schmul Publishing Company, 1988), 165.

3 *The Interlinear Greek-English New Testament* (London: Samuel Bagster and Sons Limited, 1967), 190.

4 Reverend J. G. Pike, *Counsel for Young Disciples* (New York: American Tract Society, 1823), 14.

5 Edward Kennaway Groves, *George Müller and Successors* (Bristol, UK: n.p., 1906), 360.

6 Roger Steer, *George Müller: Delighted in God* (Wheaton, IL: Harold Shaw, 1975), 132, 179.

7 G. Fred Bergin, *Autobiography of George Müller* (Bristol, UK: J. Nisbet and Company, 1914), 81.

8 Basil Miller, *George Müller, Man of Faith and Miracle* (Minneapolis: Bethany House Publishers, 1941), 85–86.

9 Albert Barnes, *Notes on the New Testament, Luke and John* (Grand Rapids: Baker, 1956), 276.

Appendices

From "The Philosophy of Fasting"
Edward Earle Purinton, 1906

Words in themselves are as futile as stray bricks. They endure only when cemented by feeling and aligned by purpose. The field of literature is mostly a dreary brick-yard, with chipped and broken bits scattered about to mark what might have been had the builder known.

Life is the only literature that lives. And if I had not first lived this book, it would never be worth the writing. *To write for any other reason than that one must is* to insult oneself and to martyr one's friends. If you write only when you must, you may not always be considerate to your friends. But you will at least be true to yourself. And the perusal of your writings can never be too hard a price to pay for knowing someone who is sincere. Sincere humans are about as common as brave gazelles or compassionate tigers.

"The Philosophy of Fasting" is a plea for human sincerity and a treatise on human wholeness. The first twenty-five years of my life I was anything but whole because I was anything but sincere. I did not dare be true to myself, or with my fellows. Civilization, classicism and orthodoxy had combined to make me appear what I was not and crucify what I was. Body, brain and soul, I was burdened with a mass of externals that weighed heavier and sunk deeper day by day until the life was almost crushed out of me.

The routine of existence was eternally maddening me—every clock, calendar and school-bell in town seemed to shriek the cruelty of law and order. The claim of senseless customs, the grasp of useless habits, the sway of rule and rote, the clutter of superfluous possessions, the onus of fictitious duties, the miasma of popular opinion the rut of precedent, the chain of environment, the blindfold of superstition—from all these barriers to human progress I was struggling to be free. The doctors meanwhile declared with oracular accent they could find no physiological basis for disease—it must be all in my imagination! Of course it was. Everything is that counts, especially a doctor's diagnosis—which counts financially.

Then came the Thirty-Day Fast. I found God through this Fast, which is equivalent to saying I found myself for we are One and the Same. During this month I ate nothing at all, drank nothing but water and occasionally acid fruit-juice. There were four objects to be achieved by means of this rather heroic measure: *Renovation, Delectation, Domination, Illumination.* All were realized. Physically, I felt that I was healthier and enjoyed everything as I had when a child. Mentally, I got a grip on myself that nothing had ever given and that nothing now can ever shake. Spiritually, I saw the heavens opened and the ultimate truths of the Infinite revealed in glorious array beyond the span of the sunrise or the gleam of the farthest star.

Fasting is not a panacea. Only Nature grants panaceas. And she makes hers fresh for each case. Nor does she employ human dispensaries. But Fasting, *rightly conducted and completed,* is nearest a panacea for all mortal ills of any drugless remedy I know, whether physiological, metaphysical, or inspirational. Fasting, resting, airing, bathing, breathing, exercising and hoping—these seven simple measures, if sanely proportioned and administered, will cure any case of acute disease. And almost any case of chronic.

I have proved to myself everything I put in print. But I'm not desirous of converting anybody else. And I haven't time to retrace the line of travel in order to describe it. So, to satisfy your brain as well as your soul—and it's just as necessary—you will be wise to take the facts offered by more patient investigators. Progress is best when it's gradual. You don't knock out all the underpinning of a house you're moving—you gently abstract one prop after another. One drawback to this book is it doesn't leave you any props at all—props medicinal, metaphysical, social, conventional, moral, theological, or otherwise respectable. And it'll be easier for you to feel them fall by degrees, with a nicety more mercifully adjusted.

In conclusion, I commend to you very earnestly not the author—not the theory—not the book; solely, utterly and everlastingly, Truth. Only when Truth and a mortal coincide does the mortal become immortal. I would not have it otherwise if I could. And my one hope is that enough of the splendor of immortality may shine through this message to light you a little farther up the steps of attainment

Proclamation Appointing a National Fast Day Washington, D.C.

March 30, 1863.

Senator James Harlan of Iowa, whose daughter later married Robert Lincoln, introduced this Resolution in the Senate on March 2, 1863. The Resolution

asks President Lincoln to proclaim a national day of prayer and fasting. The Resolution was adopted on March 3, 1863 and signed by Lincoln on March 30, 1863.

By the President of the United States of America

A Proclamation.

Whereas, the Senate of the United States, devoutly recognizing the Supreme Authority and just Government of Almighty God, in the affairs of men and of nations, has, by a resolution, requested the President to designate and set apart a day for National prayer.

And whereas it is the duty of nations as well as of men, to own their dependence upon the overruling power of God, to confess their sins and transgressions, in humble sorrow, yet with assured hope that genuine repentance will lead to mercy and pardon; and to recognize the sublime truth, announced in the Holy Scriptures and proven by all history, that those nations only are blessed whose God is Lord.

And, insomuch as we know that, by His divine law, nations like individuals are subjected to punishments and chastisements in this world, may we not justly fear that the awful calamity of civil war, which now desolates the land, may be but a punishment, inflicted upon us, for our presumptuous sins, to the needful end of our national reformation as a whole People? We have been the recipients of the choicest bounties of Heaven. We have been preserved, these many years, in peace and prosperity. We have grown in numbers, wealth and power, as no other nation has ever grown. But we have forgotten God. We have forgotten the gracious hand which preserved us in peace, and multiplied and enriched and strengthened us; and we have vainly imagined, in the deceitfulness of our hearts, that all these blessings were produced by some superior wisdom and virtue of our own. Intoxicated with unbroken success, we have become too self-sufficient to feel the necessity of redeeming and preserving grace, too proud to pray to the God that made us! It behooves us then, to humble ourselves before the offended Power, to confess our national sins, and to pray for clemency and forgiveness.

Now, therefore, in compliance with the request, and fully concurring in the views of the Senate, I do, by this my proclamation, designate and set apart Thursday, the 30th day of April, 1863, as a day of national humiliation, fasting and prayer. And I do hereby request all the People to abstain, on that day, from their ordinary secular pursuits, and to unite, at their several places of public worship and their respective homes, in keeping the day holy to the Lord, and devoted to the humble discharge of the religious duties proper to that solemn occasion.

All this being done, in sincerity and truth, let us then rest humbly in the hope authorized by the Divine teachings, that the united cry of the Nation will be heard on high, and answered with blessings, no less than the pardon of our national sins, and the restoration of our now divided and suffering Country, to its former happy condition of unity and peace.

In witness whereof, I have hereunto set my hand and caused the seal of the United States to be affixed.

Done at the City of Washington, this thirtieth day of March, in the year of our Lord one thousand eight hundred and sixty-three, and of the Independence of the United States the eighty seventh.

By President: Abraham Lincoln
William H. Seward, Secretary of State.
Source: *The Collected Works of Abraham Lincoln*, edited by Roy P. Basler.

Selected Reading

- The following books are written by authors of various theological perspectives. This list is suggested for further reading and perspective.
- Abbott-Smith, G., *A Manual Greek Lexicon of the New Testament*. Charles Scribner's Sons, New York, NY, 1956.
- Airola, Paavo O., *How to Keep Slim, Healthy and Young with Juice Fasting*. Health Plus Publishers, Phoenix, AZ, 1971.
- Alford, Henry, *The Greek Testament, Vols. I and II*. The Moody Bible Institute of Chicago, Chicago, IL, 1958.
- Alpha-Omega Ministries, Inc., *Practical Word Studies in the New Testament, Vol. 1*. Leadership Ministries Worldwide, Chattanooga, TN, 1998.
- Anderson, Andy, *Fasting Changed My Life*. Broadman Press, Nashville, TN, 1978.
- Arndt, William F., and Gingrich, F. Wilbur, *A Greek-English Lexicon of the New Testament*. The University of Chicago Press, Chicago, IL, 1957.
- Arnold, Clinton E. (ed.), *Zondervan Illustrated Bible Backgrounds Commentary, Vol. 2*. Zondervan Publishing House, Grand Rapids, MI, 2002.
- Barnes, Albert, *Notes on the New Testament—Acts of the Apostles*. Baker Book House, Grand Rapids, MI, 1953.
- _____, *Notes on the New Testament—Luke and John*. Baker Book House, Grand Rapids, MI, 1954.
- Beall, James Lee, *The Adventure of Fasting*. Fleming H. Revell Company, Old Tappan, NJ, 1974.
- Benson, Bob, Sr., and Benson, Michael W., *Disciplines for the Inner Life*. Deeper Life Press, Hendersonville, TN, 1989.
- Benson, Clarence H., *Biblical Faith*. Crossway Books, Wheaton, IL, 2003.
- Bercot, David W. (ed.), *A Dictionary of Early Christian Beliefs*. Hendrickson Publishers, Peabody, MA, 1998.
- Berry, George Ricker, *The Interlinear Literal Translation of the Greek New Testament*. Zondervan Publishing House, Grand Rapids, MI, 1963.
- Bock, Darrel, *NIV Applications Commentary*. Zondervan Publishing House, Grand Rapids, MI.
- Bright, Bill, *5 Steps to Fasting & Prayer*. New Life Publications, Orlando, FL, 1998.
- _____, *7 Basic Steps to Successful Fasting & Prayer*. New Life Publications, Orlando, FL, 1995.

- Brown, Francis, S.R. Driver and C.A. Briggs, *A Hebrew and English Lexicon of the Old Testament.* (Clarendon Press: Oxford University Press, 1957.
- Brown, George M., *Prayer Power.* 1981.
- Buksbazen, Victor, *The Feasts of Israel.* Christian Literature Crusade, Fort Washington, PA, 1954.
- Buttrick, George A., *The Interpreter's Bible, Volume 12, Isaiah.* Abingdon Press, New York, NY, 1956.
- Carnahan, Elizabeth J., *Weavings.* Upper Room Ministries, Nashville, TN, 2004.
- Chavda, Mahesh, *The Hidden Power of Prayer and Fasting.* Destiny Image Publishers, Inc., Shippensburg, PA, 1998.
- Cho, Dr. David Yonggi, *The Fourth Dimension Volume Two.* Bridge-Logos Publishers, Gainesville, FL, 1983.
- Cho, Paul Y., *Prayer, Key to Revival.* Word Publishing, Dallas, TX, 1984.
- Christopher, Hiram, *The Relations of God to the World.* Gospel Advocate Publishing Company, Nashville, TN, 1900.
- Clark, David J., Mundhenk, Norm, Nida, Eugene A., and Price, Brynmor F., *The Books of Obadiah, Jonah, and Micah.* United Bible Societies, New York, NY, 1993.
- Coffman, James Burton, *Commentary on Luke.* Firm Foundation Publishing House, Austin, TX, 1975.
- _____, *The Major Prophets—Isaiah, Vol. I.* Abilene Christian University Press, Abilene, TX, 1990.
- Colbert, M.D., Don, *Fasting Made Easy.* Siloam, Lake Mary, FL, 2004.
- Coleman, Lyman, *Ancient Christianity,* Original 1852, Republished. Forgotten Books Ltd. Dalton House, Windsor Avenue, London, 2015.
- *The Confessions of St. Augustine.* Washington Square Press, Inc., New York, NY, 1951.
- Conybeare, W.J., and Howson, J.S., *The Life and Epistles of St. Paul.* William B. Eerdmans Publishing Company, Grand Rapids, MI, 1966.
- Cott, M.D., Allan, *Fasting as a Way of Life.* Bantam Books, New York, NY, 1977.
- _____, *Fasting: The Ultimate Diet.* Bantam Books, New York, NY, 1975.
- Cove, Gordon, *Revival Now Through Prayer and Fasting.* Schmul Publishing Co., Inc., Salem, OH, 1988.
- Crabb, Dr. Larry & Allender, Dr. Dan B., *Hope When You're Hurting.* Zondervan Publishing House, Grand Rapids, MI, 1996.
- Damazio, Frank, *Seasons of Intercession.* City Bible Publishing, Portland, OR, 1998.
- Davis, John D., *A Dictionary of the Bible.* Baker Book House, Grand Rapids, MI, 1968.
- Delitzsch, F., *Commentary on the Old Testament, Vol. VII.* William B. Eerdmans Publishing Company, Grand Rapids, MI, 1969.
- Doughty, Stephen V., *Weavings.* Upper Room Ministries, Vol. XIX, Nashville, TN, 2004.
- Douglas, J.D. (ed.), *New Bible Dictionary Second Edition.* Tyndale House Publishers, Inc., Wheaton, IL, 1962.
- Duvall, Edith H., *A Believer's Thoughts.* 1906.

- Eastman, Dick, *Dick Eastman on Prayer.* Global Christian Publishers, Grand Rapids, MI, 1989.
- Eaton, Michael, *No Condemnation, A New Theology of Assurance.* InterVarsity Press, Downers Grove, IL, 1995.
- Ehret, Arnold, *Prof. Arnold Ehret's Mucusless Diet Healing System.* Ehret Literature Publishing Co., Beaumont, CA, 1977.
- Eiselen, Frederick Carl, Lewis, Edwin, and Downey, David G. (ed.), *The Abingdon Bible Commentary.* Abingdon-Cokesbury Press, Nashville, TN, 1929.
- Falwell, Jerry, and Towns, Elmer (ed.). *Fasting Can Change Your Life.* Regal Books, Ventura, CA, 1998.
- Fallows, Samuel, *Bible Encyclopedia,* Vol. II. The Howard Severance Company, Chicago, IL, 1906.
- Fee, Gordon D., *God's Empowering Presence.* Hendrickson Publishers, Peabody, MA, 2002.
- Fenhagen, James C., *A Guide to Prayer,* Upper Room, Nashville, TN, 1990.
- Ferguson, Everett, *Backgrounds of Early Christianity.* William B. Eerdmans Publishing Company, Grand Rapids, MI, 1987.
- Fernando, Ajith, *The NIV Application Commentary—Acts.* Zondervan Publishing House, Grand Rapids, MI, 1998.
- Fletcher, Dr. Kingsley A., *Prayer and Fasting.* Whitaker House, New Kensington, PA., 1992.
- Floyd, Ronnie W., *The Power of Prayer and Fasting.* Broadman & Holman Publishers, Nashville, TN, 1997.
- Foster, Richard J., *Celebration of Discipline.* HarperOne, New York, NY, 1998.
- Frahm, Anne E., and Frahm, David J., *Cancer Battle Plan.* Pinon Press, Colorado Springs, CO, 1992.
- Franklin, Jentezen, *Fasting.* Charisma House, Lake Mary, FL, 2008.
- Fudge, Edward, *Our Man in Heaven, An Exposition of the Epistle to the Hebrews.* C. E. I. Publishing Company, Athens, AL 1973.
- Gaines, Thomas. *Healthful Fasting.* Joseph F. Wagner, Inc., New York, NY, 1944.
- Gingrich, F. Wilbur, *Shorter Lexicon of the Greek New Testament.* The University of Chicago Press, Chicago, IL, 1965.
- Gore, Charles, *The Sermon on the Mount.* John Murray, London, 1900.
- Graf, Jonathan, *The Power of Personal Prayer.* Navpress, Colorado Springs, CO, 2002.
- Green, Thomas Sheldon (revised by), *A Greek-English Lexicon to the New Testament.* Samuel Bagster & Sons LTD, 4 New Bridge Street London EC 4.
- Gregory, Susan, *The Daniel Fast.* Tyndale House Publishing, Inc., Carol Stream, IL, 2010.
- Grubb, Norman, *Rees Howells, Intercessor.* CLC Publications, Fort Washington, PA, 1952.
- Gundry, Stanley N., *The NIV Application Commentary, Acts.* Zondervan Publishing House, Grand Rapids, MI, 1998.
- Guthrie, D., and Motyer, J.A., *The New Bible Commentary Revised.* William B. Eerdmans Publishing Company, Grand Rapids, MI, 1970.

- Haggard, Ted, *Liberation through Prayer and Fasting*. New Life Church, Colorado Springs, CO, 1995.
- Hagin, Kenneth E., *A Commonsense Guide to Fasting*. Faith Library Publications, Tulsa, OK, 1999.
- Hailey, Homer, *A Commentary on the Minor Prophets*. Baker Book House, Grand Rapids, MI, 1972.
- Hall, Franklin, *Glorified Fasting*. Franklin Hall, San Diego, CA, 1948.
- Hallesby, O., *Prayer*. Augsburg Publishing House, Minneapolis, MN, 1931.
- Hamblin, H.T., *A Venture of Faith*. Hamblin Pub., Chichester, England, 1928.
- Harris, R. Laird (ed.), *Theological Wordbook of the Old Testament, Vol 1*. Moody Press, Chicago, IL, 1980.
- Harris, Randall (ed.), *The Contemporaries Meet the Classics on the Holy Spirit*. Howard Publishing Company, Inc., West Monroe, LA, 2004.
- Hastings, Edward (ed.), *The Speaker's Bible—Isaiah, Vol. II*. Baker Book House, Grand Rapids, MI, 1963.
- _____, *The Speaker's Bible—Minor Prophets*. Baker Book House, Grand Rapids, MI 1962.
- _____, *The Speaker's Bible—Luke, Vol. I*. Baker Book House, Grand Rapids, MI 1961.
- Hemfelt, Robert, and Fowler, Richard, *Serenity: A Companion for Twelve Step Recovery*. Trinity Broadcasting Network, Santa Ana, CA 1990.
- Hitchcock, Roswell D., *Hitchcock's Topical Bible and Cruden's Concordance*. Baker Book House, Grand Rapids, MI, 1952.
- Hoffman, Marlin S., *The Power of Prayer and Fasting*. Hoffman Publications, Abilene, TX, 1968.
- *Holman Study Bible, Revised Standard Version*. A. J. Holman Company, Philadelphia, PA, 1962.
- Hughes, Phillip Edgcumbe, *Paul's Second Epistle to the Corinthians*. William B. Eerdmans Publishing Company, Grand Rapids, MI, 1962.
- Irwin, C.H. (ed.), *Irwin's Bible Commentary*. Zondervan Publishing House, Grand Rapids, MI, 1977.
- Jamison, D.D., Robert, *A Commentary, Critical and Explanatory on the Old and New Testaments*. The S.S. Scranton Company, Glasgow, Scotland, 1871.
- Jeremias, Joachim, *The Prayers of Jesus*. Fortress Press, Philadelphia, PA, 1967.
- Kelly, William Donald, *One Answer to Cancer*. The Kelley Foundation, 1969.
- Kenyon, E.W., *In His Presence*. Kenyon's Gospel Pub. Society, Inc., Lynnwood, WA, 1978.
- Koehler, Ludwig and Walter Baumgartner, *Lexicon in Veteris Testament Libros*. Wm. B. Eerdmans Publishing Co., Grand Rapids, MI, 1951.
- Kuyper, Abraham, *The Work of the Holy Spirit*. Funk & Wagnalls Company, New York, NY, 1900.
- Lawson, James Gilchrist, *Deeper Experiences of Famous Christians*. Warner Press, Anderson, IN, 1970.
- Leupold, H.C., *Exposition of Daniel*. Baker Book House, Grand Rapids, MI 1969.
- Lewis, C.S., *The Problem of Pain*. The Macmillan Company, New York, NY, 1962.
- Lewis, Jack P., *The Minor Prophets*. Baker Book House, Grand Rapids, MI, 1966.

- Lindsay, Gordon, *Prayer and Fasting*. Christ for the Nations, Inc., Dallas, TX, 2000.
- _____, *The Art of Successful Praying*. Christ for the Nations, Inc., Dallas, TX, 1998.
- Linn, Dr. Robert, *The Last Chance Diet*. Bantam Books, New York, NY, 1976.
- Lloyd-Jones, D. Martyn, *Studies in the Sermon on the Mount, Vol. 1*. William. B. Eerdman's Publishing Company, Grand Rapids, Mich., 1972.
- Longenecker, Richard N., *The Ministry and Message of Paul*. Zondervan Publishing House, Grand Rapids, MI, 1971.
- Louw, Johannes P., and Nida, Eugene A. (ed.), *Greek-English Lexicon of the New Testament*. United Bible Societies, New York, NY, 1989.
- Marshall, Catherine, *Something More*. Guideposts Associates, Inc., Carmel, NY, 1974.
- Martin, William C., *The Layman's Bible Encyclopedia*. The Southwestern Company, Nashville, TN, 1964.
- McBride, Alfred, *The Gospel of the Holy Spirit*. Our Sunday Visitor, Inc., Huntington, IN, 1992.
- McCasland, David, *Oswald Chambers, Abandoned to God*. Discovery House Publishers, Grand Rapids, MI, 1993.
- McEntyre, Marilyn, *Fasting*. Weavings, Upper Room, Nashville, TN, 2004.
- McGarvey, J. W., *The New Testament Commentary, Matthew and Mark, Vol. I*. Gospel Light Publishing Company, Delight, AR, 1875.
- McGee, J. Vernon, *Thru the Bible Commentary Series—Isaiah, Chapters 36-66*. Thomas Nelson Publishers, Nashville, TN, 1991.
- McGuiggan, Jim, *The Book of Isaiah*. Montex Publishing Company, Lubbock, TX, 1985.
- McKnight, Scot, *Fasting*. Thomas Nelson, Nashville, TN, 2009.
- Metzger, Bruce M., *A Textual Commentary on the Greek New Testament*. United Bible Societies, Germany, 1971.
- Milavec, Aaron, *The Didache*. Liturgical Press, Collegeville, MN, 2003.
- Miller, Madeline S., *Harper's Bible Dictionary*. Harper and Row, London, 1952.
- _____, *The New Harper's Bible Dictionary*. Harper and Row, London, 1973.
- Morley, John, *William Ewart Gladstone*. Macmillan and Company, London, 1903.
- Müller, George, *Release the Power of Prayer*. Whitaker House, New Kensington, PA, 2000.
- Murray, Andrew, *With Christ in the School of Prayer*. Bridge-Logos Publishers, Gainesville, FL, 1999.
- Nave, Orville J., *Nave's Topical Bible*. Moody Press, Chicago, IL.
- *Nelson's Quick Reference Bible Handbook*. Thomas Nelson Publishers, Nashville, TN, 1993.
- *Nelson's Quick Reference Topical Bible Index*. Thomas Nelson Publishers, Nashville, TN, 1995.
- Nicklem, Nathaniel, *The Interpreter's Bible*, Volume 2. Abingden Press, New York, NY.

- Oswalt, John N., *The NIV Application Commentary—Isaiah*. Zondervan Publishing House, Grand Rapids, MI, 2003.
- Parker, John W., *The Bible Cyclopedia*, Volume 1. London, England: West Strand, 1841.
- Peloubet, D.D., F.N., *Peloubet's Bible Dictionary*, The Religious Tract Society, London, 1925.
- Peterman, Mary E., *Healing, A Spiritual Adventure*. Fortress Press, Philadelphia, PA, 1974.
- Peterson, Robert L. and Strauch, Alexander, *Agape Leadership, Lessons in Spiritual Leadership from the Life of R. C. Chapman*. Lewis and Roth Publishers, Littleton, CO, 1991.
- Pfeiffer, Charles, *Wycliffe Bible Encyclopedia*, Volume 1. Moody Press, Chicago, IL.
- Pfeiffer, Charles F. and Harrison, Everett, F. (ed.), *The Wycliffe Bible Commentary*. The Southwestern Company, Nashville, TN, 1962.
- Pike, J. G. Counsel to Young Disciples, American Tract Society, Nassau Street, New York, NY, 1823.
- Pilcher, Joseph, *Fast Health*. Berkley Publishing Medallion Book, New York, NY, 1977.
- Pink, Arthur W., *An Exposition of the Sermon on the Mount*. Baker Book House, Grand Rapids, MI, 1977.
- Piper, John, *A Hunger for God*. Crossway Books, Wheaton, IL, 1997.
- Prime, Derek, *A Christian's Guide to Prayer*. Fleming H. Revell Company, Great Britain, 1963.
- Prince, Derek, *How to Fast Successfully*. Derek Prince Publications, Ft. Lauderdale, FL, 1976.
- _____, *Prayer and Fasting*. Fleming H. Revell Company, Old Tappan, N.J., 1973.
- _____, *Restoration Through Fasting*. Derek Prince Publications, Ft. Lauderdale, FL, 1970.
- _____, *Shaping History Through Prayer & Fasting*. Fleming H. Revell Company, Old Tappan, N.J., 1973.
- Purinton, Edward Earle, *The Philosophy of Fasting*. Benedict Lust Publisher, New York, NY, 1906.
- Pusey, Edward B. (ed.), *The Confessions of Saint Augustine*. Washington Square Press, Inc., New York, NY, 1951.
- Ray, David, *The Art of Christian Meditation*. Tyndale House Publishers, New York, NY, 1977.
- Richards, Lawrence O., *Illustrated Bible Handbook*. Thomas Nelson Publishers, Nashville, TN, 1997.
- Rinker, Rosalind, *Prayer, Conversing with God*. Zondervan Publishing House, Grand Rapids, MI, 1959.
- Robinson, George, *Isaiah, Pulpit Commentary*. Wm. B. Eerdmans Publishing Company, Grand Rapids, MI, 1950.
- Ryan, John K., *The Confessions of Saint Augustine*. Random House, New York, NY, 1960.

- Ryan, Thomas, *Fasting Rediscovered*. Paulist Press, New York, NY, 1981.
- Salmonson, Marilyn, *Fasting as unto the Lord*. Whitaker House, New Kensington, PA, 2000.
- Shepherd's Notes, *Isaiah*. Holman Reference, Nashville, TN, 1998.
- Shoemaker, Helen. *The Secret of Effective Prayer*. Word Books, Waco, TX, 1967.
- Slotki, Israel W., *Isaiah*. The Soncino Press, LTD, London, England, 1959.
- Smith, Alice, *40 Days Beyond the Veil*. Regal Books, Ventura, CA, 2003.
- Smith, David R., *Fasting, A Neglected Discipline*. Christian Literature Crusade, Fort Washington, PA, 1954.
- Smith, Kenton K. (ed.), *Standard Bible Commentary—Mark*. Standard Publishing, Cincinnati, OH, 1968.
- Smith, William, *Smith's Bible Dictionary*. A. J. Holman Company, Philadelphia, PA.
- Spence, H.D.M., *The Pulpit Commentary, Acts and Romans, Vol. 18*. William. B. Eerdmans Publishing Company, Grand Rapids, MI, 1950.
- _____, and Exell, Joseph S. (ed.), *The Pulpit Commentary, Isaiah, Vol. 10*. William. B. Eerdmans Publishing Company, Grand Rapids, Mich., 1958.
- _____, *The Pulpit Commentary, Mark and Luke, Vol. 16*. William B. Eerdmans Publishing Company, Grand Rapids, Mich., 1958.
- Stanley, Charles F., *God's Power through Prayer*. J. Countryman Publishers, Houston, TX.
- _____, *The Glorious Journey*. Thomas Nelson Publishers, Nashville, TN, 1996.
- Swope, Mary Ruth, *The Roots & Fruits of Fasting*. Whitaker House, Avinger, TX, 1992.
- *Teaching from Zion, Vol. 14*. July, 2001.
- Thayer, Joseph Henry (ed.), *A Greek-Lexicon of the New Testament*. T. & T. Clark, Edinburgh, 1956.
- *The System Bible Study*. The System Bible Company, Chicago, IL, 1922.
- Towns, Elmer L., *The Beginner's Guide to Fasting*. Servant Publications, Ann Arbor, MI, 2001.
- _____, *Fasting for Spiritual Breakthrough*. Regal Books, Ventura, CA, 1996.
- Treat, Casey, *Renewing the Mind: The Key to Transformation*. Harrison House, Tulsa, OK, 1992.
- Vine, W. E., *An Expository Dictionary of New Testament Words*. Thomas Nelson Publishers, Nashville, TN, 1985.
- Walker, N.W., *Raw Vegetable Juices*. Norwalk Press Publishers, Phoenix, AZ, 1970.
- Wallis, Arthur, *God's Chosen Fast*. Christian Literature Crusade, Fort Washington, PA, 1968.
- Walvoord, John F., and Zuck, Roy B., *The Bible Knowledge Commentary—New Testament*. Victor Books, Wheaton, IL, 1983.
- *Watchtower Bible and Tract Society of Pennsylvania*. Watchtower Bible and Tract Society of New York, Inc., New York, NY, 1995.
- Weavings, *Fasting*. Upper Room Ministries., Nashville, TN, 2004.

- *Webster's New Twentieth Century Dictionary of English Language.* World Publishing Company, Cleveland and New York, 1956.
- White, Ellen G., *Testimonies for the Church.* Pacific Press Publishing Association, Mountain View, CA, 1948.
- Wigram, George, *Englishman's Hebrew and Chaldee Concordance.* Oxford University Press, Grand Rapids., 1970.
- Wilhelmsson, John C., *The Philosophical Contributions of Edith Stein, an Academic Thesis.* San Jose State University, CA, 2016.
- Willard, Dallas, *The Divine Conspiracy.* HarperCollins Publishers, New York, NY, 1998.
- _____, *The Spirit of the Disciplines.* Harper, San Francisco, CA, 1991.
- Willis, John T., *The Living Word Commentary, Isaiah, Volume 12.* Sweet Publishing Co., Austin, TX, 1980.
- Wilson, Billy, *Fasting Forward.* Pathway Press, Cleveland, TN, 2005.
- Young, Robert, *Analytical Concordance of the Bible.* Funk & Wagnalls Company, New York.

Forty Days Fasting Journals

Stephen Lemmons

This addendum of *Worship with Fasting* is an illustration of the purpose and validity of the book itself. Each year, our son Stephen and his wife, Lynn, fast from Ash Wednesday until Palm Sunday. A number of individuals from their church and their life also fast during this period. During this fast each year, Stephen sat at his computer each day recording his thoughts and often emailing them to friends. With permission we have included 20 select entries from Stephen's fasting journals (1997 – 2017). They provide a picture of what God does in the heart of a person on an extended fast. What follows is a sample of his spiritual journey. (AGL)

Editor's Note: Because these were taken from written journals, we felt it best to leave them largely unedited. We wanted the reader to catch as much as possible Stephen's mindset when he wrote them, so we did not feel it necessary to polish them.

January 6, 2003; 11:15 PM
Preparation for a three day fast.

As we fast on January 23-25, please include in your prayers that God will burst the seams of our family at Southlake with himself. Pray for his presence to be so real and so tangible that even those on the fringes can't help but be swept up by his power and majesty. Pray that we become the house of prayer our shepherds have called us to be; that we become contagious sharing his good news, that we allow God's unlimited abilities and mighty works an avenue to be exhibited in our corners of his world.

Pray that we become real! That we continue to become what we attempt to profess to be! Pray for the homecomings that he is preparing. Pray for the spiritual awakening that is occurring to completely displace any room for Satan in any of our hearts! Pray for the fence-sitters, the appeasers, those who prefer the status-quo, to be shaken and awakened to the awesome power and abilities of the God of Abraham, Isaac and Jacob! Pray for his will, not ours, to be what we focus and expend our energies on.

Folks, I don't know if these are the end times or not. As far as I'm concerned, yesterday was a good time for the return of Jesus Christ! However, I am not, nor are you, God. He will do his thing in his time for his reasons. As long as he allows this old world to continue spinning, we must be about our Father's business. We must take a step from the comfortable to the uncomfortable. We must walk on water when the waves are breaking around us. We must learn to loosen our grip on what we can touch, smell, hear, taste and see, and learn to cling to the unseen; what is eternal! We must ask and trust him to do through us what we know we cannot do by ourselves!

Is this a difficult lesson? Who among us commands the dawn to break or the day to bow? Who among us stores up rain, or hail, or snow, or lightening; or tells the oceans where to begin and end? Who has walked the recesses of the deep, or attends as the young are born in the wild? Who has been to the top or bottom of any mountain, or ocean, or reaches of our galaxy? Who among us knows where death lives . . . and who among us have broken death's stranglehold on mankind?

Our strength is not in what we do, but why we do it. I pray that none of us become lost in that simple thought. God, through Jesus Christ and the power of his Holy Spirit are why we are who we are, and why we do what we do.

Learn it. Love it. Live it. To God be the glory!

March 14, 2004; 3:56 p.m.
Day 19

"Let the godly sing with joy to the Lord, for it is fitting to praise him. Praise the Lord with melodies on the lyre; make music for him on the ten-stringed harp. Sing new songs of praise to him; play skillfully on the harp and sing with joy. For the word of the Lord holds true, and everything he does is worthy of our trust. He loves whatever is just and good, and his unfailing love fills the earth."

"The Lord merely spoke, and the heavens were created. He breathed the word, and all the stars were born. He gave the sea its boundaries and locked the oceans in vast reservoirs. Let everyone in the world fear the Lord, and let everyone stand in awe of him. For when he spoke, the world began! It appeared at his command."

"The Lord shatters the plans of the nations and thwarts all their schemes. But the Lord's plans stand firm forever; his intentions can never be shaken. What joy for the nation whose God is the Lord, whose people he has chosen for his own. The Lord looks down from heaven and sees the whole human race. From his throne he observes all who live on the earth. He made their hearts, so he understands everything they do. The best-equipped army cannot save a king, nor is great strength enough to save a warrior. Don't count on your warhorse to give you victory-- for all its strength, it cannot save you. But the Lord watches over those who fear him, those who rely on his unfailing love."

"He rescues them from death and keeps them alive in times of famine. We depend on the Lord alone to save us. Only he can help us, protecting us like a shield. In him our hearts rejoice, for we are trusting in his holy name. Let your unfailing love surround us, Lord, for our hope is in you alone."

We are nearly half-way through this year's extended fast; and what have you learned? I have been reminded that fasting is *supposed* to be difficult. If it weren't then I would probably attempt to take the glory and credit for humbling myself before my God. Looking back, the easier days have been those days I spent with him. The more difficult days have been God's wake-up calls for me. They force me to address why I'm doing what I am doing.

The days I shake my self-righteous fist in God's face reminding him that I am voluntarily abstaining from solid food and could stop it at any time I choose are the times he smiles at me, reminds me he loves me and tells me, "There, today, your self-satisfaction is your reward. Enjoy it. Be filled by it. Be satisfied by it. And when you want to be filled, truly satisfied, come humbly to me."

Those are the times when like a child with his hand caught in a cookie jar, I ask again to be forgiven; when I ask to again be seated at his banquet table. These are the times I again call out that name that is above all names, the name that is the bread of life; the name of Jesus Christ.

It is beginning to dawn on me that God offers this incredible banquet table, set with the finest of everything imaginable and portions that will never run out. Yet I continually arrive to the feast with a stomach full of my opinions and my efforts and my wishes; I arrive with a stomach full of this world. He invites me to eat and I can only nibble. He invites me to indulge but the best I can do is pick at the food. He invites me to sit at his table but all I can do is complain about the menu.

My God, my Father, why do I continue to set these traps for myself? Why do I continue to ignore your promises and your provision? Why do I think that anything I may volunteer to do should impress you when I fail to appreciate the voluntary choice you, your son, made on my behalf? Who am I to bargain with my Creator? Who am I to attempt to cajole, ingratiate, impress or threaten the One who by merely speaking created the worlds and by breathing the word created the heavens?

Please forgive my arrogance. Please accept me again at your table. Please fill me, Lord. Please take me home. I want to go home.

March 19, 2009; 9:00 a.m.
Day 23

"Surely he took up our infirmities and carried our sorrows, yet we considered him stricken by God, smitten by him, and afflicted. But he was pierced for our transgressions, he was crushed for our iniquities; the punishment that brought us peace was upon him, and by his wounds we are healed. We all, like sheep, have gone astray, each of us has turned to his own way; and the Lord has laid on him the iniquity of us all."

I'm afraid I have sanitized and dressed up the humiliation, beating, and suffering of Christ and the crucifixion of Christ to the point where I no longer fully appreciate the pain and suffering he endured on my behalf. The polished and waxed engravings of the cross only make what he did for me farther removed and more difficult to comprehend. I think that the slightly smiling face of the dead Messiah, his head gently laid over on his right shoulder, with barely a mark visible on his body has, in a subliminal way, reworked, restored, even revised the horrible, malicious death that Jesus Christ suffered on my behalf.

So what's the danger in having the actual account of his crucifixion rewritten in my mind? At least one and possibly the most heinous is the ease with which I can rationalize my selfish and sinful behavior when in my mind, I only see a gentle man dying a peaceful and humane death. He took up my infirmities and carried my sorrows. Through him my sicknesses are healed. Because of what he endured, my iniquities have been removed. Because of his willingness to die in my place, I am given the opportunity to spend eternity with God.

The cross, then, with all of its horrors is the rainbow in eternity's sky of God's wish for me to live with him forever. It is the fulfillment of God's promise to provide the means to save the world, Jesus is the final ark; the "once and for all" salvation for mankind. But it is also a symbol of how inadequate I am. It is the symbol of his love and mercy. It is the reminder of grace satisfying its own requirement for justice. It is the instrument that brought his plan of salvation to me. By paying the price that I owed, he has given me the opportunity to be a child of his: not because of my talents or ingenuity or abilities, but because of his!

If someone asks him, "What are these wounds on your body?" he will answer, "These are the wounds I was given at the house of my friends." And he could look at me, because I shouted for his crucifixion. If someone asks him, "What are these wounds on your body?" he will answer, "These are the wounds I was given at the house of my friends." And he could look at me, because I testified against him. If someone asks him, "What are these wounds on your body?" he will answer, "The wounds I was given at the house of my friends." And he could look at me, because I was in command of the whip. If someone asks him, "What are these wounds on your body?" he will answer, "The wounds I was given at the house of my friends." And he could look at me, because I fashioned the crown of thorns. If someone asks him, "What are these wounds on your body?" he will answer, "The wounds I was given at the house of my friends." And he could look at me, because I not only brought the nails and the hammer to Golgotha, I swung the hammer that so securely fastened him to that cross.

I was the jeering crowd. I was the source of the hurled insults and mockery, the spit and the slaps. I gambled for his robes and cursed and laughed as he struggled to carry his cross up that hill. My hands laid the best palm branches I could find or buy one day and threw rocks and dirt at him another. My voice sang his praises one day and called for his death another.

And as I hurled my insults and ridicule, "Jesus, being in very nature God, did not consider equality with God something to be grasped, but made himself nothing, taking the very nature of a servant, being made in human likeness. And being found in appearance as a man, he humbled himself and became obedient to death-- even death on a cross! Therefore God exalted him to the highest place and gave him the name that is above every name, that at the name of Jesus every knee should bow, in heaven and on earth and under the earth, and every tongue confess that Jesus Christ is Lord, to the glory of God the Father."

March 15, 2011; 1:20 p.m.
Day 7

Exodus 32:30-34; "The next day Moses said to the people, 'You have committed a terrible sin, but I will return to the Lord on the mountain. Perhaps I will be able to obtain forgiveness for you.' So Moses returned to the Lord and said, 'Alas, these people have committed a terrible sin. They have made gods of gold for themselves. But now, please forgive their sin-and if not, then blot me out of the record you are keeping.'"

"The Lord replied to Moses, 'I will blot out whoever has sinned against me. Now go, lead the people to the place I told you about. Look! My angel will lead the way before you! But when I call the people to account, I will certainly punish them for their sins.'"

God didn't destroy the nation of Israel because Moses interceded on their behalf. However, because God is Holy, Moses knew that punishment would be required for the actions of "these people." And although punishment is always a requirement for sin, forgiveness is always an option for the sinner. But did you hear what Moses said to God? "But now, please forgive their sin—and if not, then blot me out of the record you are keeping." Moses is telling God that if he can't forgive what these people did, to just send him to hell with the rest of them! While Moses was enjoying a (true in every sense of the word), mountain-top experience, those he was chosen to lead were at the very least, breaking Commandant One of the very law Moses carried in his arms.

I don't think any of us would have faulted Moses had he said, "Go ahead, God! Rain down fire and brimstone on their heads!" But Moses didn't say that. Instead, he interceded on behalf of the children of Israel. Not only did he intercede, he was willing to carry the consequence of the sins of others to spare those who sinned against God.

Moses was one of the "giants" we read about in the Bible, but, if you'll remember, his mountain-top experience came after violating some of the very commandments that he was now carrying in his arms. So much for the need to be perfect before we can approach God, or before God will like us.

I believe many of us have not yet been convicted by our own sin. How can we stand in the gap for others when our own sin is ever before us? How can we continue to ignore what we know to do, or continue to participate in what we know we should run from? How can we charge the throne room of our Creator and ignore what he wants placed on his altar? Rationalize it, dress it up, put a fresh coat of paint on it, call it something more appeasing to the ear, but sin is sin. And God can have nothing to do with a heart that possesses unconfessed sin.

God doesn't ask for my perfection, but only my permission. He only asks that we be willing to allow him to use us to his glory. After all, if God could only use us once we're perfect, there wouldn't be anyone (this side of heaven) available for him to use! Perfection, or, a works-based salvation, requires that I do everything, and I mean everything. So if any of us could attain religious perfection, what was the point of God sending Jesus Christ to suffer the terrible, sadistic death that he died? It would be nothing but over-kill. No, God knew before the creation of everything that none of us could approach him by our own goodness or through our good works.

Our God, and our Salvation, who are we that you would remember us and be kind to us? Almighty One, who are we that you should show us any mercy, or grace, or favor? Father, who are we, when compared to you, that you would be mindful of us? We are your sheep; the ones always looking for the hole in the fence. We are the ones always complaining that the grass is greener in some other pasture. We are the ones who turn up our noses at the taste of the water from the streams to which you lead us. We are the ones who too quickly point out the spots and blemishes of those around us. We are the ones who say we want to be led, but more often want to lead.

Our Provision, we thank you for smiling at us and leading us and saving us from ourselves. We thank you for searching for us when any of us is absent from your sight and for not abandoning us to our "wisdom" and curiosities. I thank you because you know when I am with you, and I praise you for pursuing me when I am missing.

Please continue to shape us and mold us into what you want us to be. Please continue to help us quit trying: to stop caring about where in your wisdom you may lead us. We just want to be who you created us to be, and we only want to be where you want us to be. I want to be with you. May it be so, and amen.

April 15, 2011; 11:33 a.m.
Day 38

Revelation 11:15-19: "Then the seventh angel blew his trumpet, and there were loud voices shouting in heaven: "The whole world has now become the Kingdom of our Lord and of his Christ, and he will reign forever and ever." And the twenty-four elders sitting on their thrones before God fell on their faces and worshiped him. And they said, "We give thanks to you, Lord God Almighty, the one who is and who always was, for now you have assumed your great power and have begun to reign. The nations were angry with you, but now the time of your wrath has come. It is time to judge the dead and reward your servants. You will reward your prophets and your holy people, all who fear your name, from the least to the greatest. And you will destroy all who have caused destruction on the earth. Then, in heaven, the Temple of God was opened and the Ark of his covenant could be seen inside the Temple. Lightning flashed, thunder crashed and roared; there was a great hailstorm, and the world was shaken by a mighty earthquake."

Revelation 15:1-4: "Then I saw in heaven another significant event, and it was great and marvelous. Seven angels were holding the seven last plagues, which would bring God's wrath to completion. I saw before me what seemed to be a crystal sea mixed with fire. And on it stood all the people who had been victorious over the beast and his statue and the number representing his name. They were all holding harps that God had given them. And they were singing the song of Moses, the servant of God, and the song of the

Lamb: "Great and marvelous are your actions, Lord God Almighty. Just and true are your ways, O King of the nations. Who will not fear, O Lord, and glorify your name? For you alone are holy. All nations will come and worship before you, for your righteous deeds have been revealed."

Revelation 16:5-7: "And I heard the angel who had authority over all water saying, "You are just in sending this judgment, O Holy One, who is and who always was. For your holy people and your prophets have been killed, and their blood was poured out on the earth. So you have given their murderers blood to drink. It is their just reward." And I heard a voice from the altar saying, "Yes, Lord God Almighty, your punishments are true and just.""

What will you take away from your fast? Will you focus on and remember those days that required God's provision and sustenance, or will you only remember the difficulties of those few days? Will your thoughts and comments praise the God of Eternity or will your thoughts and comments praise you for what God did through your time with him? The God who sustained us when we were not eating is the same God who sustains us when our stomachs are full and satisfied.

I am afraid many of us will forget that He Who Is, lives within us and longs for us to continue depending on him, talking to him, praising his provision and his ability. Sadly, because we are human beings, our natural response is to run to and praise and worship what comforts us and empowers us. Because without him we are nothing, I'm afraid our stomachs and cravings will again begin moving him out of our hearts, and our plans and abilities will again become the objects of our affections.

I was recently asked how it would feel to be back to normal. Normal is where I was this time yesterday; and today I feel I am running back to what is abnormal: me and mine, what I want and what I can do, or not do, or what I can get away with. On a personal note, today is my most difficult day because I know me and I know that each bite, each meal, every choice will move me further from the intimacy I was able to enjoy with him these last few days. The best way, and the worst way, I know to describe it would be how I would feel should I make plans to cheat on Lynn. Today, I can define "normal" as what God's plans are for me; being able to close my eyes and walk heaven's streets of gold. Being able to close my eyes and see myself on my face in that incredible throne room. Being able to appreciate that God answers my prayers according to his sovereignty and his wisdom. I pray that this time next week and this time next month, I am still "normal."

My Lord, if my plans stand between you and me, take my plans! My Lord, if my stomach stands between you and me, please take my stomach! My Lord, if my cravings, or my imagination, or my inability to trust you, or my ideas of how things should be; anything that keeps me from allowing you to be God in my life...*whatever* it may be, please take it away from me! I only want to be yours! I am tired of trying to be me! I want to only be yours!

My Provision, I don't want this intimacy to end! I don't want to forget the comfort of your lap or the feel of your arms around me! I don't want the sound of your heartbeat to fade from my hearing! I don't want the smell of you to fade from my nostrils! I don't know how to pray this prayer, my Salvation and my Sustainer! I want to come home! I want this time of focusing on you to continue. I want to continue to see your throne room, and join the creatures saying, "Holy, holy, holy is the Lord God Almighty, who was, and is, and is to come." I want to continue to hear the elders say; "You are worthy, our Lord and God, to receive glory and honor and power, for you created all things, and by your will they were created and have their being." I want to stay in your presence. I want to keep looking at you. I thank you for remaining faithful to me, your unfaithful spouse. I praise you for remaining faithful to me, although I continue to prove how unfaithful I am to you. And I pray that I will not so quickly forget you and return to my own vomit; my prostitution of who I should be and what I should be about, but that I will be continually reminded of your greatness, your omnipotence, your faithfulness and your love.

Almighty God, all you have ever asked of your people is that we be honest with you and transparent with each other. I pray for the boldness and courage to be who you created me to be. When I present myself to you, and when I present myself to my family, may I only be honest and sincere.

Finally, I thank God for each of you, for your support, for your words of encouragement, for your prayers and your heart for God.

[My prayer for you:] "When I think of the wisdom and scope of God's plan, I fall to my knees and pray to the Father, the Creator of everything in heaven and on earth. I pray that from his glorious, unlimited resources he will give you mighty inner strength through his Holy Spirit. And I pray that Christ will be more and more at home in your hearts as you trust in him. May your roots go down deep into the soil of God's marvelous love. And may you have the power to understand, as all God's people should, how wide, how long, how high, and how deep his love really is. May you experience the love of Christ, though it is so great you will never fully understand it. Then you will be filled with the fullness of life and power that comes from God. Now glory be to God! By his mighty power at work within us, he is able to accomplish infinitely more than we would ever dare to ask or hope. May he be given glory in the church and in Christ Jesus forever and ever through endless ages. Amen."

March 27, 2012; 10:46 p.m.
Day 35

I exalt my God while I excuse myself. I lean on God as I depend on me. Some days I believe it is because of Jesus Christ that my sins are forgiven, and some days I live as if because of my good works, God has reason to forgive me. I am who I am because that is how God created me; true. But I am who I am because that is what I choose to be.

Where does joy come from? Does joy come from ritual or relationship? Do I do what I do because it is expected, or because it is "time," or because I should? If so, I have already received my reward from any of the rituals I have and will participate in. Ritual requires my attention to detail. Relationship requires my focus on God. Ritual dictates the "when" and "where" of what I do. Relationship dictates the whom and why of what I do. Ritual tells me how to do it. Relationship moves me to want to do it. Rituals do not save. My relationship with God does save. My rituals bring me a sense of control. My relationship with God brings a smile to his face.

Ritual causes me to focus on my needs. Relationship demands that I focus on the needs of others. Ritual means that I'm secure in crossing all of my t's and dotting all of my i's. Relationship means I have no t's to cross or i's to dot. Ritual means my efforts save me. Relationship means I am saved by God's grace through the blood of Jesus Christ. Ritual tells me to carry nails and a hammer. Relationship shows me those hands and feet. And then, all I can do is lay down my instruments of ritual and fall on my face.

On my best day, my good deeds can't touch that; forget any of the days that have been among my worst! So why do I still find myself making sure I have done everything the way it is supposed to be done? And what if someone else's ritual differs from mine; what then? Who is correct? Which is more worthy? Why do I still see my sacrifices as "Abel" offerings and see someone else's sacrifices as "Cain" offerings? How can I be sure that my understanding is the "correct" understanding? And since under the law, my salvation depends on my "correctness," I had better be dead-on with all of it.

Maybe that is why we are so quick to throw bricks at each other; in the pretense of love, because we understand that our good works and understanding may not be enough. Maybe, down deep, I recognize that my understanding and knowledge may be an incomplete understanding or knowledge. Maybe, if I can make you think like I do, then I can feel more secure in my stances. After all, there is comfort in numbers, and if you agree with me, then I must be correct.

But salvation comes from God and not through how well I keep the law, or my understanding, or my resolve, or my intentions. Therefore, my rituals can't save me. God, through Jesus Christ saves me and pardons me, day after day after day. If it were more than that, how could those who were saved in the early days of the church truly have been saved when they didn't have the Epistles or Gospels on which to disagree? Is it possible that Jesus Christ is enough and I've complicated it?

So, do I still think I can merit God's favor through my good works? Do I still think that through my efforts and intentions I can pin God's arm behind his back? Except for accepting his gift of salvation, I have no part in my redemption. He offers, and I accept...or I don't. There is no middle ground on this one. Either I am saved through faith or I can save myself. And I know me. I can't save myself. To think otherwise cheapens the horrible death that Jesus Christ endured for me and makes what he did salvation-for-hire.

> "There is a fountain filled with blood, drawn from
>   Immanuel's veins
> And sinners plunged beneath that flood, lose all their guilty
>   stains
> Lose all their guilty stains, lose all their guilty stains
> And sinners plunged beneath that flood, lose all their guilty
>   stains
> Dear dying Lamb, thy precious blood shall never lose its
>   power
> Till all the ransomed church of God be saved to sin no
>   more
> Be saved to sin no more, be saved to sin no more
> Till all the ransomed church of God be saved to sin no
>   more
> E'er since by faith I saw the stream thy flowing wounds
>   supply
> Redeeming love has been my theme, and shall be till I die
> And shall be till I die, and shall be till I die
> Redeeming love has been my theme, and shall be till I die."

My God, please forgive my arrogance. You didn't find it necessary to consult me when you created rocks, so who am I to tweak your plan for salvation; the plan that has been since eternity? Please accept my heart. It is all I have to offer. Please accept my heart and restore me.

February 14, 2013; 10:01 a.m.
Day 2

The way I deal with God is, I guess, the way I sometimes think my kids deal with me. Give him the nod when you think he expects a nod. Give him the choice when he expects that choice. Give him the attitude when he expects that attitude, respect when respect is in order. Talk to him when he seems determined to talk. Ask for $20 expecting a $20 but hope for $10. How can I maximize the returns on my smallest investment? How much is too much and how little is enough? Now I don't mean to bust on my kids; after all, they are children . . . still experiencing life, still learning lessons the hard way. Still, sometimes, it seems, going-along to get-along. I get that. But I don't have that excuse. Although my actions and attitude may sometimes contradict this next statement, I am no longer a child.

The way I think my children sometimes deal with me is maybe because of the way they have seen me deal with my God. During my holy-of-holy days, he gets my nod. During my choose-what-I can do without, or choose-what-I-know-he-would-want times, he is the easy choice. When my bills are paid and my stomach is full, I can stand and raise my hands in praise with the best of them. As long as our health and happiness can stand little, if any improvement, I'm thanking him for his blessing, and will ask that he continue to keep my boat from being rocked. I'll even give him 10, 15 percent to get his attention, because I won't really miss it.

In treating him this way, I guess I expect God to go-along so that he and I can continue to get-along. After all, look at all I have done for him. He is lucky to have me. When I think he needs a nod, he's got it. When I actually stop to consider what choice he would have me make, I'll give it to him. I'll cry during worship. I'll give what I won't miss. I'll slow down for the encounters he places in my day as long as it serves us both. I'll pray the easy prayers, call evil, choice, look to tomorrow to save me from today and go-along to get-along. And, I'll continue to be a child.

Well, and God help me, no longer. If it will bring glory to my Father, I want my boat to be rocked this year. If it will help my relationship with him become more intimate and close and dependent, start the waves now. Will I sink, will I swim or will I walk on water? I don't know and I don't care. Because he wants to be my true refuge, because he asks my permission to be my protection, because God is my fortress, I say "Bring it."

"So, if you think you are standing firm, be careful that you don't fall! No temptation has overtaken you except what is common to mankind. And God is faithful; he will not let you be tempted beyond what you can bear. But when you are tempted, he will also provide a way out so that you can endure it."

"Submit yourselves, then, to God. Resist the devil, and he will flee from you. Come near to God and he will come near to you. Wash your hands, you sinners, and purify your hearts, you double-minded. Grieve, mourn and wail. Change your laughter to mourning and your joy to gloom. Humble yourselves before the Lord, and he will lift you up."

"I love you, Lord, my strength. The Lord is my rock, my fortress and my deliverer; my God is my rock, in who I take refuge, my shield and the horn of my salvation, my stronghold."

So, God, you know me. You know I trust you to provide the basics, but depend on me to provide what I think is truly needed. You know that I truly believe you looked me in the eye at that point of eternity when you decided to create, knowing, and already sacrificing what my choices would require of you. You know I call you Sovereign and at the same time will challenge your authority. You say, "Love me," and I respond with, "How much?" You say, "My grace is sufficient." and I say, "It better be." You say, "Come to me and rest," and I say, "As soon as possible." You say you have set a table with the best of the best, and all I can do is pick and choose and complain about your provision. Because, too often, I arrive at your table full of myself, bloated with my ambitions, stuffed full of my own ideas, I have no room available to sit in your company and eat from your table.

Father, empty me. Strip me. Break me. Just please don't leave me. And on those days when I walk away from you, please follow me far enough to stay within my view, so I'll know how to find my way home, again.

February 18, 2013; 9:26 a.m.
Day 6

I wasn't there when the earth's foundations were laid. I wasn't there when its dimensions were marked off or the measuring line was stretched across it. I have never given orders to the morning or shown the dawn its place. I have never journeyed the springs of the sea or walked in the recesses of the deep. I have never seen where death lives. I don't know where light and darkness reside. I have not been to the storehouses of snow or hail. I have not seen the place where lightening is dispersed or where the winds come from... but I know someone who has and he allows me to crawl up in his lap and call him Father.

I don't think we can out-think and thereby out-pray what he wants to do through us and for us. Our God is a God of the radical, the called-out. He is a God of extravagance. Don't think so? Think of the peacock or the birds of the tropical forests; think of a sunset or a snowfall, a raging river, a baby's cry, the speed of a cheetah, the stars at night, the waves in the oceans.

Do you need more? Try this for extravagant: "In him we have redemption through his blood, for the forgiveness of sins, in accordance with the riches of God's grace that he lavished on us with all wisdom and understanding." "...that he lavished on us with all wisdom and understanding." "...that he lavished on us with all wisdom and understanding." Still unconvinced? How about this; "Very rarely will anyone die for a righteous man, though for a good man someone might possibly dare to die. But God demonstrates his own love for us in this: While we were still sinners, Christ died for us. Since we have now been justified by his blood, how much more shall we be saved from God's wrath through him!" I serve an extravagant God!

I serve a God who has to be itching to pour his Holy Spirit into this world, this continent, this country, this state, this city, this neighborhood, this street, this house, this vessel. I serve a God who said through his Son, "Which of you, if his son asks for bread, will give him a stone? Or if he asks for a fish, will give him a snake? If you, then, though you are evil, know how to give good gifts to your children, how much more will your Father in heaven give good gifts to those who ask him!"

So, as I see things this morning, here is my spiritual death-spiral. I keep myself so anesthetized and soothed I am too comfortable to think God needs to do anything for me. I spend so much time and expend so much energy ensuring I am anesthetized and soothed that I ignore or completely miss the real needs around me. Because I am so comfortable and don't think there is anything God really needs to do for me, and I don't see the needs around me, why bother him? Why go to all the pain or discomfort of getting on my knees in my closet? After all, if I'm okay and, from what I "see," those around me are okay, there are other things we could do with our time.

And, then, when I do pray they tend to be the prayers of someone completing a nightly pre-landing checklist. No real passion (I have everything I need); no real praise (I haven't been, and look where I am); no real confession (after all, don't forget, I'm okay), no intercession (after all, everyone else is doing fine, too). Even with the Holy Spirit doing his best to intercede on my behalf as I recite my prayers, I am certain the best he can do is, "Uh, he said he's going to bed now, I-I-I think."

And since I don't get on my face in that throne room, lay it on the line and test him, Malachi 3:10, he goes without my praise, I go without his blessing and countless situations and circumstances around me go on and on with no divine intervention.

Father, thank you for the glimpse into your throne room you are allowing us. Thank you for filling us with your Holy Spirit and for the incredible feeling that gives us. Thank you for allowing me, the one who applied the final blow when the nails were being driven in your Son's hands and feet, a place at your table, a robe and the promise of an eternity on my face in your throne room praising your name!

Father, help me trade my physical hunger for a hunger for you and a hunger for the lost. As my body resists and screams out, help me trade those aches and pains for an aching for those that need your mercy and grace. Help me actively seek them. Help me go out of my way to find them.

Help me step out of my comfort zone and embrace mankind. Give me the courage to become who you created me to be. Help me be your son on this earth. In his name, and to Your glory, amen.

February 27, 2013; 3:30 p.m.
Day 15

So, why was God such a demanding and jealous God in the Old Testament? Why would he demand so much from those in the Old Testament and then give me his Son? Why would he tell Abraham to offer Isaac yet not stop Eli's sons from being taken from him? Why would Moses write one whole book of nothing but rules and regulations yet not be allowed to enter the Land of Promise? Why would God harden the hearts of some yet allow David the opportunity of reconciliation? I think it has to do with ownership and perception.

Whether a title, deed or license, as owner, I have the moral authority to decide what will happen with what I own. Does the right of ownership not allow me to change the color of the walls in my house? Does the right of ownership not allow me to change the landscaping in my yard? With ownership, do I not have the right to change the layout of our furniture, the layout of my office, the arrangement of all the stuff in my garage; the right to decide whether to keep or discard anything that is mine?

So too, God has the right of ownership of his creation. Sure, the differences are drastic: the color of the walls in my home compared to life; the landscape in your yard compared to life; the stuff in my office or garage when compared to life are hugely different. But if I, as owner of anything, have the moral authority to decide what goes and what stays, how much more does God have that same moral authority over everything and anything created? As my Creator he is also my owner. Not just because he created me, but even more, because he bought me, he redeemed me. God reconciled me to himself with the gift, no, with the remedy of his own design in a remedy of his own choosing. He sent himself to reconcile me to him. At that point of eternity when he decided to create me, God became the title-holder of me.

As Everlasting to Everlasting, God does what he does for his God reasons and for his God purposes. As Redeemer, Alpha and Omega, our All in All, God works with us and through us to his ends and for his results. He has the moral authority to do whatever he chooses. He has the moral authority to design and dictate his outcomes in our lives. So it isn't really about how God changed his tactics in how he deals with his creation, but, I think, more about how his creation chooses to see its interaction with him. Am I pressed down, or is God reshaping me? Am I being stepped on, or is he lifting me up? Am I running on empty, or being filled? Will I perceive God's actions through the lenses of political correctness, or accept his working in my life because he is sovereign?

My glorious God, why do I continue to attempt to weigh and judge your ways? Why do I continue to second-guess your plans? Why do I continue to dissect your word in an attempt to understand why you do all you do? As my God, as my Creator, as my Redeemer, I see now you have every right to do whatever you choose. Hold back the sun, make the rivers run dry, take the earth out of its orbit, stop the rain; just don't stop loving and reconciling me to you. Take my house, take my job, take my health; just please never stop watching for my return to you, just please never stop reaching for me or loving me. Take anything of mine you choose; it is all yours anyway. Take anything of mine you choose; I know I'll spend eternity with any of it that is important. Take anything of mine you choose, and draw me closer to you. In the name of the voice that broke the silence when he said, "Let there be Stephen," amen.

P.S. When I wrote "In the name of the voice that broke the silence when he said, "Let there be Stephen, amen.," I didn't mean it like, "Hmm, we've made the sun and the stars and the oceans, and that's all good stuff. I have an idea! Let's make Stephen!"

Sometimes my fingers run ahead of ability to read how things could come across. Please accept my apologies for how that line could read. I just meant that at some point, God said, "Let there be Stephen." And it was so.

March 1, 2013; 7:46 a.m.
Day 17

Is God really God of my life? Do my actions promote his kingdom, or do I only promote my plans for myself or my agenda? Do I allow his will to unfold in my life or, like water seeking the lowest level, is God's will for me tested with each decision I make, forced by my desires to wind its way this direction and that direction throughout my heart and throughout my day, doing its best to seek a receptive place in me to reside? Do my attempts to please, assuage and satisfy myself put me on the throne of my heart and relegate God to some self-approved corner of my life; that self-appointed piece of who I am where I will grant him audience to hear his call for me? Have I given God myself, or do I expect him to make do with the bones I choose to toss him?

If I am to be honest, too often I only allow the "dust" of God's will for me to settle where it may and only cover me in those areas of my life that I decide. So how can God be God of my life if I continue to tell him the parts of my life in which he may have a foothold while refusing him access to those parts of my life that I choose to keep for myself? How can God be God of my life if my motives and my prayers ask him to join my plans for me rather than allowing him, and them, to circumcise my heart, causing me instead to ask that I may join him in his plans for me? How can God be God of my life when my preferences and my idols will not allow him the proper place he deserves in my heart and in my life?

"The one sitting on the throne was as brilliant as gemstones--jasper and carnelian. And the glow of an emerald circled his throne like a rainbow. Twenty-four thrones surrounded him, and twenty-four elders sat on them. They were all clothed in white and had gold crowns on their heads. And from the throne came flashes of lightning and the rumble of thunder. And in front of the throne were seven lampstands with burning flames. They are the seven spirits of God. In front of the throne was a shiny sea of glass, sparkling like crystal."

"In the center and around the throne were four living beings, each covered with eyes, front and back. The first of these living beings had the form of a lion; the second looked like an ox; the third had a human face; and the fourth had the form of an eagle with wings spread out as though in flight. Each of these living beings had six wings, and their wings were covered with eyes, inside and out. Day after day and night after night they keep on saying, 'Holy, holy, holy is the Lord God Almighty--the one who always was, who is, and who is still to come.'"

"Whenever the living beings give glory and honor and thanks to the one sitting on the throne, the one who lives forever and ever, the twenty-four elders fall down and worship the one who lives forever and ever. And they lay their crowns before the throne and say, 'You are worthy, O Lord our God, to receive glory and honor and power. For you created everything, and it is for your pleasure that they exist and were created.'"

My God, "Oh, that you would rip open the heavens and descend, make the mountains shudder at your presence--as when a forest catches fire, as when fire makes a pot to boil—no one has ever imagined, no ear heard, no eye seen, a God like you who works for those who wait for him."

My Provision, "As the deer pants for streams of water, so I long for you, O God. I thirst for God, the living God. When can I come and stand before you? Day and night, I have only tears for food, while my enemies continually taunt me, saying, 'Where is this God of yours?' Why am I discouraged? Why am I so sad?" "I will put my hope in you, oh God! I will praise you again--my Savior and my God! But why am I discouraged? Why so sad? I will put my hope in God! I will praise you again--my Savior and my God!"

My Hope, for your love, for your sacrifice, for you, I thank you. My Salvation, for your mercy, for your grace, for you, I worship you. How much longer will I attempt to be you? How much longer will I try to tell you how to do your job? How much longer before you take me home? In the name of my Salvation, my Redeemer and my friend; Jesus Christ, amen.

March 4, 2013; 9:50 a.m.
Day 20

John 17, "When Jesus had finished saying all these things, he looked up to heaven and said, 'Father, the time has come. Glorify your Son so he can give glory back to you for you have given him authority over everyone in all the earth. He gives eternal life to each one you have given him. And this is the way to have eternal life--to know you, the only true God, and Jesus Christ, the one you sent to earth. I brought glory to you here on earth by doing everything you told me to do. And now, Father, bring me into the glory we shared before the world began. I have told these men about you. They were in the world, but then you gave them to me. Actually, they were always yours, and you gave them to me; and they have kept your word. Now they know that everything I have is a gift from you, for I have passed on to them the words you gave me; and they accepted them and know that I came from you, and they believe you sent me.'"

"My prayer is not for the world, but for those you have given me, because they belong to you. And all of them, since they are mine, belong to you; and you have given them back to me, so they are my glory! Now I am departing the world; I am leaving them behind and coming to you. Holy Father, keep them and care for them--all those you have given me--so that they will be united just as we are. During my time here, I have kept them safe. I guarded them so that not one was lost, except the one headed for destruction, as the Scriptures foretold."

"And now I am coming to you. I have told them many things while I was with them so they would be filled with my joy. I have given them your word. And the world hates them because they do not belong to the world, just as I do not. I'm not asking you to take them out of the world, but to keep them safe from the evil one. They are not part of this world any more than I am. Make them pure and holy by teaching them your words of truth. As you sent me into the world, I am sending them into the world. And I give myself entirely to you so they also might be entirely yours."

"I am praying not only for these disciples but also for all who will ever believe in me because of their testimony. My prayer for all of them is that they will be one, just as you and I are one, Father--that just as you are in me and I am in you, so they will be in us, and the world will believe you sent me. I have given them the glory you gave me, so that they may be one, as we are--in them and you in me, all being perfected into one. Then the world will know that you sent me and will understand that you love them as much as you love me. Father, I want these whom you've given me to be with me, so they can see my glory. You gave me the glory because you loved me even before the world began! O righteous Father, the world doesn't know you, but I do; and these disciples know you sent me. And I have revealed you to them and will keep on revealing you. I will do this so that your love for me may be in them and I in them."

The only observation I can make about this prayer is how incredibly short of Christ's prayer for unity, perseverance and faith in him I fall. And it isn't in some big way that I continue to miss what he prayed for, but in so many subtle ways.

Unity is easy when I decide with whom I should be united. You must look like I look and act like I act and live in my kind of neighborhood before I will take notice of you. Then you must think like I think and agree with me and have the same temperament as I do before I will accept you. And then you must worship like I worship and pray like I pray and interpret scripture like I do before I can be united with you. Me, you, me, you, me, you; until finally... God isn't to be found in any of my relationships. Only you and I are in my relationships. And if we are to be honest, we are operating from similar preferences and prejudices. You are wrestling for the upper hand in our relationship just as I am. And don't just ignore that statement. Think about it.

Is it possible for me to look at you like God looks at you? What would happen if you accepted me for who I am, and not what you want to make of me? What if we both understood that the ground beneath the cross is level; that here, there is no upper hand to be had? What if I decide to pay more attention to the blood that soaks the ground here than to expend my energy attempting to change you? What if I decide to concentrate more on the labored, irregular breathing of the One who hangs there in front of both of us than telling you what God meant in his word for you? Since the Holy Spirit cannot lead two hearts that are sincerely seeking God into disunity, what if we both decide to focus on God and the sacrifice that he provided and decide to love each other as we find each other? And by so doing, agree to leave it up to him to perfect both of us? Unity is his prayer for us. Will we continue to berate and shout each other down, or will we instead focus on the blood we profess is our salvation? Unity isn't in me looking like you or you acting like me. Unity is in his blood.

March 5, 2013; 8:31 a.m.
Day 21

It's true: most of the time, my heart is led around by my head. And although that isn't always a bad thing, I end up in ruts. Everything from daily routines to what I wear to how I respond to folks around me to how I provide for my family, for the most part, is because for most of the year, my head leads my heart. Because of that, I have to make a conscious decision to say "no" to this, and to say "yes" to that. I have to make the daily decision to wear Christ into my day or to wear myself into my day.

My head isn't bad or evil. It's just that it has learned what needs to be done and has determined the most efficient way to accomplish what needs to be done. It has learned what gets me through my day and has identified those things that only complicate my day. It doesn't care about the encounters that God may place in my day, because to it, those encounters don't always help me accomplish what needs to be accomplished. It doesn't have the eyes to see the needs of others because it is focused only on my needs. It doesn't want to be the arms and legs and feet of Jesus to others. That's why I tithe, it will tell me. It doesn't want to slow down to smell the roses or look a child in the eye as they try to tell me about losing their first tooth, because it will tell me, the roses will fade and the kid will eventually lose 19 more teeth; give or take a couple. My head doesn't want me to stop to ponder the universe, to consider the complexity of creation, or its Creator, because, it will tell me, it is what it is. And my head will indulge choices that I make that move me away from God because it serves its purposes in getting me through my day. My head tries to convince me that a little sin is okay.

For most of the year, almost like a tolerated spouse, my heart takes its cues from my head. My heart tries to speak up, and does from time to time, only to be put back in its place. Oh sure, there are times that my heart will prevail; those times when my head realizes that it could benefit from what my heart is suggesting; those times when it sees there is something to be gained; those times when it goes-along to get-along. But, if I am to be honest, sadly, most of my year will find me being lead around by my head.

This is one of the reasons I do this each year. For a time, some years for days and some years for a few weeks, my head takes direction from my heart. My heart directs my thoughts and my actions. "Those" decisions that I must fight on a daily basis aren't even decisions to be made during these days. I don't wake up to the decision of whether or not to wear Christ into the new day because yesterday, I didn't take him off. My eyes are open. My grip has let go of the things that my head insists that I grasp--which means my hands are free to be held by my Salvation.

March 12, 2013; 9:43 a.m.
Day 28

Lynn and I are considering taking our family to Honduras on a mission trip this summer. One of the things we are expected to prepare and submit prior to the trip is our testimony. So it got me to thinking, what is my testimony? If I have to stop and think about it, my testimony may be different than it should be. My testimony isn't just something I say, rather, shouldn't it be who I am? Job 15 says, "Your own mouth condemns you, not mine; your own lips testify against you." And in Jeremiah 14, "Although our sins testify against us, O Lord, do something for the sake of your name. For our backsliding is great; we have sinned against you."

So, my testimony, my life, is what is supposed to be salt, leaven and a light on a hill. My testimony, my life, is what my children witness during periods of stress and disappointment as well as times of victory and celebration. My testimony, my life, is what my co-workers see when the deadline is approaching and the project isn't complete. My testimony, my life, is what employees and employers see when I could choose to cut corners, or exaggerate an expense report. My testimony, my life, is what my neighbors witness on Thursday night and Saturday afternoon, not just Sunday morning. My testimony, my life, is how I interact with clerks, attendants, shop owners and even government office personnel. My testimony, my life, is how I respond to those in a bigger hurry than traffic will permit, those that break in the line that I have been standing in for an hour, how I respond to my enemies, and those considered to be unlovable.

What I do does speak louder than what I say. Too often, my children can't hear what I am saying because my actions are deafening. Too often, my neighbors, co-workers and friends can't hear the good news of Jesus I attempt to speak because they are being shouted-down by what they see me doing. Too often, those seeking seek elsewhere, those hurting continue to hurt; the sick go unhealed by the blood of the Lamb because what is witnessed in me is no different than what they see in themselves. And why would they want more of the same? My testimony, my life, should be Jesus Christ and him crucified. Period.

I need to remember this as I live my life and as I interact with the rest of the world. If I don't stand out, then I wonder if I really am sold out. If my walk and talk are no different from those I'm around, I'm probably on the wrong path. If my actions blend in with those around me, then my salt is most likely wet and my light is probably out.

Have I been viewing God's grace as a heavenly enabler: the gift that allows me to keep one foot in Jerusalem and one foot in Babylon? I need to call on God, through faith, and allow God's grace to dry out my salt and reignite my light. I need to stand out. I need to be different. And then, hopefully, those around me will be able to hear what I say by seeing what I do.

March 13, 2013; 10:47 a.m.
Day 29

Today is going to be a praise and worship day. The longer I sat here, the more what I thought was on my heart left me and the more verses of praise and worship kept coming to me. So, in taking a dose of my own medicine, I'm not asking God to join me in my plans for today, I am joining him in his plans for today. I hope you have a blessed day.

Shout with joy to God, all the earth! Sing the glory of his name; make his praise glorious! Say to God, "How awesome are your deeds! So great is your power that your enemies cringe before you. All the earth bows down to you; they sing praise to you, they sing praise to your name." Come and see what God has done, how awesome his works in man's behalf!

He turned the sea into dry land, they passed through the waters on foot--come, let us rejoice in him. He rules forever by his power, his eyes watch the nations--let not the rebellious rise up against him. Praise our God, O peoples, let the sound of his praise be heard; he has preserved our lives and kept our feet from slipping. Come and listen, all you who fear God; let me tell you what he has done for me. I cried out to him with my mouth; his praise was on my tongue. If I had cherished sin in my heart, the Lord would not have listened; but God has surely listened and heard my voice in prayer. Praise be to God, who has not rejected my prayer or withheld his love from me!

For he will deliver the needy who cry out, the afflicted who have no one to help. He will take pity on the weak and the needy and save the needy from death. He will rescue them from oppression and violence, for precious is their blood in his sight. Praise be to the Lord God, the God of Israel, who alone does marvelous deeds. Praise be to his glorious name forever; may the whole earth be filled with his glory. Amen and Amen.

Praise the Lord. Sing to the Lord a new song, his praise in the assembly of the saints. Let Israel rejoice in their Maker; let the people of Zion be glad in their King. Let them praise his name with dancing and make music to him with tambourine and harp. For the Lord takes delight in his people; he crowns the humble with salvation. Give thanks to the Lord, for he is good; his love endures forever.

Praise be to the Lord, the God of Israel, from everlasting to everlasting. Let all the people say, "Amen!" Praise the Lord.

March 14, 2013; 9:59 a.m.
Day 30

I truly believe I have to rethink my priorities. I am told by everything from newspapers to magazines to movies to television, radio, billboards, bumper stickers, friends and foes;-even the U.S. Mail, that I have to go for the gusto, that I should live for today; that I shouldn't just want it, that I need it. I am told that in order to be popular, successful, fulfilled and part of the "in" crowd, I should step-on, walk-through and run over anyone or anything that stands between me and whatever today's latest status symbol may be.

As a practicing follower of Christ, have I bought into the idea that as long as I list God as my first priority--God, country, family, job--I have some sort of heavenly dispensation for continuing to be blinded by Madison Avenue's glitz and glamour? That as long as God is listed as priority one, I can chase the stuff and acquire the fluff that Hollywood tells me I must have? That as long as God is listed as my number one priority, my energies and efforts may be aimed at whatever I choose? After all, God is my number one priority, right?

The truth is, whatever my priorities are, (or, whatever I think they may be), if they are anything other than God and his righteousness, I have ignored what he would have me be about and I have given myself an excuse to not excel in any of my priorities. Matthew tells us, "But seek first his kingdom and his righteousness, and all these things will be given to you as well." It doesn't say seek his kingdom and his righteousness, then your family, then your job, then your whatever. I have looked and looked and can't find anywhere in the Bible where I am told to pursue anything other than God and his righteousness. By dividing my time between three or four top priorities, I don't successfully pursue any of them, often to the detriment of all of them.

If my sole priority is God and his righteousness, I believe by default I will be the best husband and father I can be. If I focus on chasing and catching God and his righteousness, I believe I will be the best employee, employer and witness for him that I can be. By focusing on multiple priorities, am I attempting to perform some spiritual slight-of-hand parlor trick that permits me to excel at none of my priorities because I'm chasing all of them? And since I don't excel at any of them, I can't hold myself accountable for missing any of them. After all, God and his grace will cover my shortcomings, right? By no means am I telling God what his grace will and will not cover, but verses like James 4:17, "Anyone, then, who knows the good he ought to do and doesn't do it, sins," makes it difficult to continue thinking I can focus on multiple priorities and fall short in all of them.

So again, "seek first his kingdom and his righteousness, and all these things will be given to you as well" and, "Anyone, then, who knows the good he ought to do and doesn't do it, sins." I can no longer afford to divide my priorities. My relationship with God can no longer afford to be satisfied with being in the top three or four. He must be the one and only one.

March 18, 2013; 9:46 a.m.
Day 34

In God's timing, when the angel of life finally comes for me, I'll spend the first few hundred thousand years on my face in that incredible throne room. I read that the saints of God are the only ones who can stand in that throne room, and I'll be fine with being on my face. And so the angels and the elders and the beasts won't have to teach me the songs that we read about in the book of Revelation, I'm trying to memorize them all now. I know that those times I've been in his lap in my dreams won't come close to what heaven will actually be like. But scripture does say, "Now to him who is able to do immeasurably more than all we ask or imagine, according to his power that is at work within us, to him be glory in the church and in Christ Jesus throughout all generations, for ever and ever! Amen." And in order for hm to do immeasurably more than I can ask or imagine, I have to ask and I have to imagine.

I want to hang out with my grandparents and then spend the next couple hundred thousand years fishing with my Papa. I want to see him walking around in his new body. I want to run my hand over his bald head again. I want to hold his hand again. I want to sit with Mema as she tries to teach me how to crochet and I want to tell her again that I love her. I want to get to know my grandfather. And I want to go with him into the forest to fell trees. I want him to teach me how to plow behind mules. And I want to work with Grandmother in her new garden. And this time, I will pay attention when she tries to give me advice on how and when to plant or tries to give me her recipe for fried-pies or squirrel and dumplings. And I want to run and play with my sister, Darla. And I want to walk over, what is to my dad and me, our promised land. I want to sit on the banks of Tumbling Creek with him and watch as the cattle of a thousand hills graze. And I'll remind my mom that in this place, we don't have to worry about injury or illness; that in this place we can have chocolate cake for breakfast. And when the time is right, I want my daughter, Emily, to teach me how to dance on God's great dance floor.

And I want to just sit with Job. I want to talk to David. I love his Psalms because I see myself in so many of them. From mountain tops to ocean depths back to mountain tops. And I won't mind standing in line. I want to tell Adam and Eve that even if they hadn't messed things up, I did. I want to ask Moses if being denied his promised land in his lifetime was worth his possession of the land in his new life. I want to ask Abel if he saw it coming. I want to tell Elisha, nice job. That when raising children, sometimes it doesn't take a village, but two bears. I want to just sit and observe Abraham. I want to ask the new earth if its groaning and waiting was worth all the destruction and recreation that I caused it. I want to see the tree of life. I want to follow Gabriel around and I want to ask him if he is the one I talked to at the singles retreat so many years ago. I want to laugh with Jeremiah. I want to hug Hosea, who through his story helped me see who I am. I want to meet Joshua and Caleb and thank them for their testimony and faith. I want to meet Joseph and thank him for his example of persistence and trust in God. I want to hang out with Isaac, Jacob and Esau, and a fellow-lefty, Ehud. I want to find Jonah, and I promise I won't make fun of him. I want to compare notes with John and tell Peter how much I appreciate his example of what it looks like to be a practicing follower of Christ. I want to thank Paul for his words that challenge and convict, but offer freedom and release at the same time. I want to meet the other thief who confessed Jesus Christ, the Samaritan woman from the well, and the woman caught in the act of being used. I have a lot in common with each of them.

I want to ask Ignatius, Quirinus and Hernes, and their families, Justin, Rhais and her mother, Marcella, who in A.D. 201 had boiling pitch poured over their heads and were then set on fire, where faith in the face of fire comes from. I want to meet the legion of Roman soldiers who all being Christians and refusing to bow to Rome, were ordered to kill every tenth man within the legion in the expectation that those remaining would recant. But when those remaining wouldn't renounce their faith in Jesus Christ, a tenth of those were ordered killed at the hand of the legion. And so on, and so on, and so on, until the last one remaining had to be put to the sword by those watching. Because of their faith, the entire Roman legion was wiped away from this earth, yet through that brutal act, were swept to their heavenly reward.

To the young mother, who after being turned over by her husband because of her faith, watched as each of her four children were killed in front of her, then endured having her unborn child ripped from her womb, yet still refused to deny the One who is unseen, but made up her very existence. Paraphrasing, she told her children, "Hush, and when we next awake, we will greet each other in the place where pain is no more."

"Therefore, since we are surrounded by such a great cloud of witnesses, let us throw off everything that hinders and the sin that so easily entangles. And let us run with perseverance the race marked out for us, fixing our eyes on Jesus, the pioneer and perfecter of faith. For the joy set before him he endured the cross, scorning its shame, and sat down at the right hand of the throne of God. Consider him who endured such opposition from sinners, so that you will not grow weary and lose heart."

My God, my Creator, my Sustainer, my Provider, to Your glory, for Your reasons, because You Were, You Are, and You Are To Come. And I'm ready when you are.

March 22, 2013; 9:20 a.m.
Day 38

There is some heavenly line that not even God will cross. It can be found somewhere between what my heart sings to him and why I do what I do. Paul said it better; "I can anticipate the response that is coming: "I know that all God's commands are spiritual, but I'm not. Isn't this also your experience?" Yes. I'm full of myself—after all, I've spent a long time in sin's prison. What I don't understand about myself is that I decide one way, but then I act another, doing things I absolutely despise. So if I can't be trusted to figure out what is best for me and then do it. It becomes obvious that God's command is necessary."

"But I need something more! For if I know the law but still can't keep it, and if the power of sin within me keeps sabotaging my best intentions, I obviously need help! I realize that I don't have what it takes. I can will it, but I can't do it. I decide to do good, but I don't really do it; I decide not to do bad, but then I do it anyway. My decisions, such as they are, don't result in actions. Something has gone wrong deep within me and gets the better of me every time."

"It happens so regularly that it's predictable. The moment I decide to do good, sin is there to trip me up. I truly delight in God's commands, but it's pretty obvious that not all of me joins in that delight. Parts of me covertly rebel, and just when I least expect it, they take charge. I've tried everything and nothing helps. I'm at the end of my rope. Is there no one who can do anything for me? Isn't that the real question? The answer, thank God, is that Jesus Christ can and does. He acted to set things right in this life of contradictions where I want to serve God with all my heart and mind, but am pulled by the influence of sin to do something totally different."

That phrase, "this life of contradictions," is where I'm going. It is the difference between what God sees in my heart and what he sees from my actions. It is what he hears my heart sing to him one moment and hears my mouth say the next moment. It is what God knows I want to do and be and become compared to what I so often act out. It is my soul begging to be in his lap, begging for him to bring me home, still wrapped up in a body that seems to do everything possible to keep me as far away as possible from the intimacy I so much want with him. And there, I believe, is where the fine line is.

God, being the merciful God that he is, prefers the song of my heart to everything else he has seen me do. God, being Never-Failing and Ever Faithful, walks up to that line that even he won't cross, the line between my ability to choose him or myself, and with love and patience and grace and pardon and mercy and kindness and understanding and empathy, gently places his hand under my chin and lifts my head. He lifts my head! And when my eyes finally meet his eyes, I can see the compassion he has for me.

He knows I am broken, and he asks to mend me. He knows I am ashamed, and he offers to take my shame. He knows I am afraid, and he comforts me in only the ways that he can. He knows that my fears often drive my choices, and he asks that I lay it all down on the same shoulders that carried my cross to Calvary. He knows that I too often act out of impulse, and he asks to protect me. He knows that my selfishness and self-sufficiency and my pride are attempts to deal with my pain on my own, and he asks me to give it all to him.

He knows I want to honor him. He knows I want to serve him. He knows I want to live for him. And there is no condemnation in his eyes. There isn't any judgment in his eyes. There isn't anything but acceptance and yet knowing all about me, he still lifts my head and tells me that he loves me. And that I belong to him. And he reminds me that he will never leave me. "But you are a shield around me, O Lord; you bestow glory on me and lift up my head."

A couple of house-keeping issues. First, depending on the type and duration of your fast, be careful how you break your fast. Time in the throne room will take on a whole new meaning for you if you ignore this. Second, I've been asked by several what I'm most looking forward to when the fast is over. The best way I can describe planning to end my fast would be how I think I would feel if I were planning to cheat on Lynn. It took me so long this year to reach my a-ha day, and now I'm purposefully planning to end it. And it needs to be done. God won't be honored if I go beyond what I committed to him in prayer during my preparation time. But still, I think it's what planning on cheating would feel like. But to the question, anything that requires a knife, fork, bread, a grill, or any kind of barbeque sauce or marinade, on the rare side of medium rare, and doesn't require a spoon, a bowl and isn't a broth, soup or juice.

Also, I appreciate the kind responses I received from so many of you this year. Your prayers and words of encouragement helped me through some tough days. Some years I wonder if sending out my journal is more like folks slowing down to look at a really bad wreck on the interstate. But because of your questions and responses, I was encouraged and lifted up on days when I most needed prayer, assurance and encouragement. And for those concerned, I don't have a death-wish, but a life-wish. I am not a physical being having an eternal experience, but an eternal being having a physical experience. And I know that God will come for me in his own sweet time. But there's nothing wrong with reminding him that I'm ready when he is.

And finally, "My response is to get down on my knees before the Father, this magnificent Father who parcels out all heaven and earth. I ask him to strengthen you by his Spirit—not a brute strength but a glorious inner strength—that Christ will live in you as you open the door and invite him in. And I ask him that with both feet planted firmly on love, you'll be able to take in with all followers of Jesus the extravagant dimensions of Christ's love. Reach out and experience the breadth! Test its length! Plumb the depths! Rise to the heights! Live full lives, full in the fullness of God. God can do anything, you know—far more than you could ever imagine or guess or request in your wildest dreams! He does it not by pushing us around but by working within us, his Spirit deeply and gently within us.

Glory to God in the church! Glory to God in the Messiah, in Jesus! Glory down all the generations! Glory through all millennia! Oh, yes!" And amen.

March 25, 2013; 10:54 a.m.
Day 41

This morning I was looking for something to make my landing a little easier. Not physically, but emotionally. Physically, I'm good. But I woke up at 3:30 this morning with all of my normal doubts and fears: should've, would've, could've back in their proper places. That's what breaking a fast does for me. Right or wrong, I don't know. But it always happens. Something to do with wearing my Provision into my day or wearing my provision into my day, I guess. Anyway, I was looking for something to remind me that although I am not, He IS, and I came across the links below. Make sure you have just under 10 minutes to watch them, and be prepared to be blown away. I can't find anything on-line about who these kids are.

For the last 13 years, and after sending my journal out over 14 extended fasts, I've never sent an email out on day 41, but I'm considering it. In a day when adults can't get to church until after the second song is underway, and if kids come at all, they come wearing last night's chips on their shoulders (not all, but a lot of them), it's so refreshing to run across these kids singing the "oldies." Singing to my heart. Slowing my fall. Helping to direct a softer landing.

I love you. And so far, so good as far as my landing. Be blessed by what follows. And as always, to his glory, and for his purposes.

[Note: Links cannot be provided. Do YouTube search for "children singing hymns."]

March 17, 2016; 5:22 p.m.
Day 37

In previous years I have compared preparing to break my fast with what it would feel like if I planned to cheat on Lynn. I won't retract that because in previous years, that's the only way I could imagine how it would feel. But not this year. This year it is more a recognition that today I'm in the safe arms of my Salvation, and that this time next week I still can be. That he is God and I am not. That reconciliation is his and repentance is mine.

In previous years, I was working and fighting, pushing and denying myself in attempts to earn an audience with him. And although I often said I wasn't attempting to ingratiate myself to him, I guess I was. He still always showed up and carried me safely home, but I'm certain only after several forehead smacks. By the way, besides the holes in his hands and feet, if Jesus has a flat spot on his forehead, it's my fault.

Considering breaking this year's fast is more like preparing to go home from some really great time away from home. I won't sever anything with each bite, as I felt in previous years. But, where I find myself, and him, is when he is always there offering himself to me. I only need to offer myself to him, not try to earn my way to him. Not attempt to cajole or corral or ingratiate myself to him; no. I just need to be me and allow him to be him! And although I know that the insights and revelations, the intimacy and security I find today are brighter and more visible today than they will be in June, that doesn't mean they won't still be available to me. Not because of anything I've done, but because of what he has already done. Because that's just who he is! He is a great Father! He is a great God! He lets me drink from a well I didn't dig and welcomes me to the shade of trees that I didn't tend! He feeds me from vineyards I didn't plant and topples cities and armies ahead of me! He runs to meet me when he sees me coming home and clothes me and puts his ring on me! He is more concerned with me being home than where I've been. He is more concerned with our reconciliation than with what separated us. Love wins.

Another short one today. What matters, matters, and what doesn't matter doesn't matter. There's nothing else to say.

March 18, 2016; 1:12 p.m.
Day 38

Well, this is it. Have you ever been somewhere that you didn't want to leave? That's where I am. I am at peace. I am at rest. I am loved. I am his. I am in his arms, his embrace. And although it takes me doing this to find myself here, this year he met me on day one, reminding me of all the ditches he towed me from, scooped me up and hasn't let me go. But, I know that meal after meal, bite after bite, I will lose some of where I find myself today. And that's ok, because he will be there, that he is always there. And because of him, this year, I've reconciled myself with myself and more importantly, because of Jesus, we are reconciled. He has forgiven my attempts to be him. And, I have forgiven myself of my attempts to be him. My best arguments are met with "love wins." And therein lies part of the problem . . . "my . . ." So, love wins. That may be too easy or simplistic or dismissive for some, but love wins. Love wins doesn't mean there aren't consequences to choices and actions. But it means that love wins. And who am I to deny any who seek reconciliation and reunion when that is what I have been shown? The consequences of my actions and choices put him on that cross. But still, he runs to meet me with his robe and his ring! He still offers me water and shelter! How can I respond any differently?

Housekeeping: Depending on the type and duration of your fast, be careful how you break your fast or "time in the throne room" will take on a completely different meaning. (Sorry, but there aren't many fasting jokes you can make!) The size of your stomach and the enzymes in your stomach have changed drastically since you began. Small bites and small portions of light, easily digested foods for the first few days will better serve you. It took you several days to get here, so don't expect to dine at your favorite steak, chicken or Mexican restaurant for the first few days. And like when you began your fast, if and when your body tells you to go, go. You may think you are Superman and can ignore this warning, but if you do, make sure you have a change of costume with you.

Finally, this may be the last year that I do this. I appreciate all the prayers and responses I've received from so many of you this year and over the past years. However, this year God finally got through to me. Love wins. Love wins. No matter how I try to tweak and manage life, no matter how I think I should react or respond, he has finally gotten through to me. Love wins.

I hope to start preparing our garden late next week. I don't have the strength or energy to do it now; but the garden hopefully will welcome my little garden-helper and create some deep, rich roots in our relationship. I may send some before, during and after pictures, but probably that will be the last you'll hear from me. Just remember to live well and to love well because--all together, love wins. God wins. And I'll see you on the other side.

About the Author

Albert Lemmons is a national senior advisor on the Presidential Prayer Committee, and is an accomplished author and teacher, whose works have been read widely. He is also a member of the Denomination Prayer Leaders Network.

He is well-known for his prayer enrichment seminar on prayer and faith. In the last 50 years, Lemmons has conducted over more than 600 10-hour weekends on this subject going to every continent but Australia.

Lemmons, who is now in his 65th year of ministry, comes from a family that has been a part of the Churches of Christ for nearly 200 years. At the age of 16, he began his pulpit ministry every Sunday in a small community of churches and preached his first funeral when he was 17.

Today, Lemmons continues to conduct seminars, mainly in the states, encouraging cooperation and a sense of community. Throughout his 65 years of ministry, Lemmons said the most important thing he has learned is that Jesus is always the answer and he continues to find inspiration in a deeper relationship with Him.